GABRIEL GARCÍA MÁRQUEZ

GABRIEL GARCÍA MÁRQUEZ
THE LAST INTERVIEW
and OTHER CONVERSATIONS

edited and with an introduction by DAVID STREITFELD

MELVILLE HOUSE
BROOKLYN · LONDON

First Melville House printing: January 2015

Melville House Publishing   8 Blackstock Mews
145 Plymouth Street   and   Islington
Brooklyn, NY 11201   London N4 2BT

mhpbooks.com   facebook.com/mhpbooks   @melvillehouse

Library of Congress Cataloging-in-Publication Data
García Márquez, Gabriel, 1927-2014.
  Gabriel García Márquez : the last interview and other conversations ; introduction by David Streitfeld.
    pages   cm
    ISBN 978-1-61219-480-6 (pbk.) – ISBN 978-1-61219-481-3 (ebook)
    1. García Márquez, Gabriel, 1927-2014–Interviews.
    2. Authors, Colombian–20th century–Interviews. I. Title.
  PQ8180.17.A73Z46 2015
  863'.64–dc23
  [B]
                                                    2014043499

Printed in the United States of America
10 9 8 7 6 5 4 3 2 1

CONTENTS

INTRODUCTION

DAVID STREITFELD

Everyone said it was like getting an audience with the pope. As in: Don't even bother trying. If Gabriel García Márquez has something to say, he can publish it himself and get worldwide attention. Why would he filter his comments through you?

I was the literary correspondent for *The Washington Post*, young and full of beans, scorning anything but the best and greatest. I revered García Márquez, as much for the scale of his accomplishment as for the actual texts themselves. *One Hundred Years of Solitude* was, as a perceptive critic once said, like a brick through a window. It let in the real life of the street, the noises and colors and sensations, and presented magical events—a trail of blood flowing across town and into a house, careful to avoid staining the rug; flowers from heaven—so straightforwardly they seem believable. Suddenly all the stories in Latin America were written in its shadow. *Solitude* was the most famous novel in the world, and perhaps the last (leaving aside the rather extra-literary case of *The Satanic Verses*) to have a demonstrable effect on it.

Letters were faxed, entreaties were made, publishers were begged. Finally the word came: Present yourself at the house in Mexico City on this date at this moment in the afternoon, and the maestro will entertain your questions. It was late 1993. García Márquez was making the transition from revolutionary firebrand to elder statesman. His recent works, *Love in the Time of Cholera* and *The General in His Labyrinth*, had extended his reputation beyond *Solitude*. He never made public appearances in the United States even though the new president, Bill Clinton, was reportedly a big fan. His elusiveness cemented the legend.

My spoken Spanish was weak, and while García Márquez was rumored to understand English quite well, he cannily refused to speak it. I came equipped with an excellent interpreter and a small gift, the newly published Library of America editions of Herman Melville. García Márquez insisted I inscribe them. I wondered if he thought I had somehow written them.

His office was behind his house in a separate bungalow, a comfortable but not overly lavish place to write, read, and hide. One wall was covered with books in at least four languages. The fiction—Lewis Carroll and Graham Greene, but also writers as contemporary as Tobias Wolff—coexisted with a dictionary of angels, worn medical texts, a map of the Paris métro, biographies of obscure statesmen, and other necessities of a working library. Another wall had compact discs and a top-notch stereo system.

Dressed all in white and looking very well fed, García Márquez was a dead ringer for the Pillsbury Doughboy. I was circling my first question, something that would straddle the line between assertive and respectful, when he interrupted. "Carlos Fuentes strongly encouraged me to talk to you," he said.

No doubt. After thirty-five years, Fuentes was still the impresario of Latin America literature. He loved brokering attention for his friends, which included everyone in the literary and diplomatic worlds.

I began again, but again García Márquez interrupted. "I don't do interviews anymore, but Jorge Castañeda said this must be an exception." I had never met Castañeda, the author of *Utopia Unarmed: The Latin American Left After the Cold War* and an influential political theorist, but clearly my renown had reached far indeed. I nodded and started for a third time.

"The Mexican ambassador in Washington is a huge fan of your work," García Márquez said, as if merely stating the obvious, like the sun had come up this morning.

I was used to being flattered by writers, to being told I was a Mozart of the pen. They routinely and without em-

barrassment offered up half-baked praise to people profil-
ing them in the hopes of securing a halfway good notice.
In that last moment before the Internet allowed writers to
cut out the middleman and train the spotlight directly
on themselves, reputations were still in the keeping of the
media.

This, however, was a master class. Unbidden, a movie
abruptly played out in my mind's eye: Mr. Ambassador, waiting by the embassy gate at six a.m. for a copy of the *Post*,
hastily grabbing it from the delivery boy, and paging through,
looking for my byline. Not finding it, he throws the paper
down and returns, sulkily, to bed.

García Márquez's message was clear: You're lucky to be
here, and I'm lucky you're on my side. After such supplica-
tion, who could ask brutal questions?

A year or two later, I went to a lecture by Castañeda. Afterward, I went up to my great admirer, a copy of his book
in my hand. He asked who I was so he could sign it, and
I carefully identified myself. He betrayed no flicker of rec-
ognition.

With García Márquez, I was more amused than taken
in. Once he finally let the interview get underway, he was as
illuminating and charming as I expected him to be. He loved
above all else talking about the books he was writing. More
than most authors, he tried not to repeat himself, even as he
got older and the temptation to revisit triumphs must have
been acute. Anyone else would have written *One Thousand
Years of Solitude*, taken the money, and ignored the inevitable
thrashing by reviewers.

Nor was he ever in a hurry. The story he discussed at length with me would not be published for more than a decade, as *Memories of My Melancholy Whores*. As it turned out, that brief tale was his last published work of fiction, although a mutual friend told me that García Márquez was playing around on his computer in the early years of the new millennium and found a lengthy tale he had finished and forgotten. I presume it will be published one day.

What interviewers want from their subjects, of course, is action, not just words. One of García Márquez's favorite stories about interviewing was the time many years earlier when a Spanish journalist wanted to talk to him. He invited her to tag along as he and his wife, Mercedes, went shopping, had lunch, and did other mundane things around Barcelona. At the end of the day, the reporter asked again for an interview—never realizing he had already given it to her. He told her—sweetly, no doubt—to get a different job, because she wasn't cut out for journalism.

If García Márquez had ever really offered such opportunities, those days were by now gone. We never moved from the couch. But he remained amusing and expansive until the end, as if I were a good friend he hadn't seen in years. Then I reminded him that we were coming back the next afternoon. His face fell. How long, he seemed to be thinking, must I be charming to these Americanos?

To soften the blow, the next day I brought my girlfriend along. García Márquez was famous even among the Latins for preferring the company of women. The interpreter from the previous day had a conflict, so Lisa and I waited outside the hotel for the highly regarded American journalist who would serve that day. And waited. Finally, an hour late, the fellow—let's call him Gringo—showed up, full of swagger. "Traffic here is horrible," Gringo explained. "Everyone is late all the time. No one cares. Don't worry."

The journey to García Márquez's house was endless. I felt that gnawing pit in my stomach of a disaster in the making. Finally we arrived and were ushered in. The maestro was understandably peeved, and perhaps only the sight of Lisa prevented him from throwing us out. He warned us that he was leaving soon for an appointment. I later learned that punctuality was a virtue he prized.

We sat down on the couch again. I asked a simple warm-up question. How was the movie he had seen the night before? Gringo stumbled over the translation. García Márquez answered, "It was good," and Gringo could not figure out what he was saying. I realized with growing horror that despite his eminent position with a leading U.S. newspaper, Gringo did not actually know more than a few words of Spanish. García Márquez was equally frustrated. The stories about him secretly understanding English were just that, stories.

I persevered, sticking to simple subject-verb-object sentences. But on the second day, there was no magic show. We saw a tired, grumpy old man. I cut it short, which he appreciated, but asked some questions about Castro, which he did not. He hated being asked about Castro, which was the one thing his U.S. fans held against him. His only mellow moments came when he flirted with Lisa.

García Márquez did few interviews in subsequent years, at least for English-language publications. I like to think it was my fault.

But he did talk to me again.

I was friendly with Patricia Cepeda, the daughter of one of García Márquez's friends back in the hungry days of Barranquilla, when he was just beginning to write and living in a whorehouse. Álvaro Cepeda died young but achieved immortality as a character in *Solitude*, whose manuscript Patricia kept in a safe deposit box.

In 1997, García Márquez and I met with Patricia as interpreter. The setting this time was more public. We went to a well-known bookstore café in Washington, D.C., Kramerbooks & Afterwords. It was late morning. Washington, then as now, was not a place where people idled during the day, so the café was almost empty. The few slackers present did not look up from their cappuccinos. Their loss.

Perhaps because of Patricia's calming presence, I saw a third García Márquez not performing, not hassled, but truly relaxed. He loved to tease. I brought a few rare editions of his books, and he said I couldn't afford them on a journalist's salary and what was I going to do when the money was gone? Did I think he, the author of these books, was going to bail me out? He also said I was preoccupied with death, and when I had written up the first interview I tried to make it look like it was his preoccupation, not mine, which is an old trick. He pretty much nailed me there.

I saw him other times after that, more casual encounters. The last time was on Rodeo Drive in Beverly Hills, where he was taking an afternoon stroll while Mercedes was browsing in one of the ultra-fashionable shops. He joked that he should go home and write something to pay for her purchases. Still mortified by Gringo's actions, I apologized again for him. (A few years later, Gringo won a Pulitzer prize, although not for writing about Mexico.)

In his sunset years, García Márquez did not feel compelled to say or publish anything at all. During one of his last public appearances, a radio reporter shoved a microphone in his face. "If I give you an interview I have to give an interview to everyone," García Márquez patiently explained. The reporter was put out, as reporters so often are, and García Márquez tried to soften the blow. "I love you, young man," he said.

García Márquez died in 2014, after several years of what is euphemistically termed "declining health." I marked the occasion by rereading an early story, "The Handsomest Drowned Man in the World," a stunning parable of the way art exalts the most ordinary of lives. It is one of his greatest works, and I think the only time I surprised him in hours of interviews was when I told him so. "But it's a story for kids," he said.

The second evening in Mexico City, he sent us off to a nearby restaurant. The food isn't great, he said, but you will have a good time. It was cavernous and dark, lit with torches on the walls and candles on the tables. The waiters fussed in a sympathetic way, and there was more silverware than I knew what to do with. They broiled an orange at the table, turning it very fast over a flame to make a sweet coffee concoction. I had succeeded in what I had set out to do, and felt giddy enough to levitate. It was like being inside a García Márquez story, placed there by the master himself. Although the food, as he said, wasn't very good.

A NOVELIST WHO WILL KEEP WRITING NOVELS

INTERVIEW BY ALONSO ÁNGEL RESTREPO
EL COLOMBIANO LITERARIO, COLOMBIA
1956

TRANSLATED BY THEO ELLIN BALLEW

By now, the name Gabriel García Márquez is probably familiar even to those who read the daily paper but never pick up a novel. Newspapers have covered the story of *Leaf Storm* (*La Hojarasca*), which received such a favorable critical response, with a zealousness befitting its status as the greatest literary achievement our country has seen in months. It is our belief that the history of the novel will be divided into two eras: before *Leaf Storm*, and after—so completely does it transcend all that's preceded it.

When we learned that he was in Medellín for his job as a journalist—García Márquez is a staff writer for the newspaper *El Espectador*, where he published the popular series that recounted in a distinctively novelistic manner the experiences of a seaman named Velasco[*]—we couldn't resist trying to interview him, in hopes of asking a few questions about his literary life, his interests, his reading.

We called to request a meeting and soon found ourselves

---

[*] The reference is to García Márquez's series of articles about the shipwreck of a Colombian Navy vessel and the sole survivor, Luis Alejandro Velasco, later translated into English and published as *The Story of a Shipwrecked Sailor*, Knopf, 1986.

shaking hands with the author of *Leaf Storm* at seven at night in the lobby of Hotel Nutibara, as he was finishing up a conversation with the racing cyclist Ramón Hoyos, perhaps as part of his assignment for *El Espectador*.

Gabriel García Márquez, cordial and unaffected, asked that we follow him to his room on the eighth floor. We liked him immediately. After taking off his jacket and loosening his tie, he was ready to answer our questions.

A NOVEL WITHIN A NOVEL

"We've read that you spent five years writing *Leaf Storm*," we say. "Is that true?"

"It is and it isn't . . . I began writing a novel in 1950. It wasn't the *Leaf Storm* that ended up being published. In the time just before 1950, I was working on a novel I called *La Casa* (*The House*). I was trying to write something like a history, you might say a biography, about a house, through the generations of people who lived there, because of course the house alone, without its inhabitants, was not an idea that lent itself to development. Still, in that first novel, I saw the house as the main character, and its inhabitants were something like the 'motors,' or what imbued this work about the life of a house with action . . . In the end I'd filled up many notebooks and I worked out that if I published them they'd make a book with some seven or eight hundred pages . . . I decided to cut it down . . . I threw out about three or four hundred pages . . . When I set to work writing the new pages that would complete the novel, I suddenly discovered an idea within the original idea, an idea that I thought might develop independently from the first one, that would form a new novel entirely. And I surrendered myself to that idea. When I first started, I thought the boy in *Leaf Storm* would tell the novel's entire story in monologues, but when I began writing I felt I needed another character, the mother of the boy, and later still another, which turned out to be the colonel. This explains the number of characters there are in the novel— three, not counting the hanged man, the doctor described in the monologues of these characters. This is why I think the process of writing *Leaf Storm* could be called spontaneous; that is to say, I just let it saunter out onto the paper as it came to me, and I hadn't drawn up any plan. Of course I was trying to do something like what Faulkner does in *As I Lay Dying*, where he has all his characters express themselves beautifully in interior monologues, and, maybe because he has so many characters, to prevent the reader from getting lost in the novel, notes the name of the speaker before each monologue begins."

He's been speaking clearly, in a polite and convincing tone. We've put our cigarettes out and he orders some drinks for us, using the phone sitting on an illuminated table. As he pours his Coca-Cola into a cup, he comments, "I don't drink alcohol, except once every seven years!"

And he continues, while finishing his soda, "I've been surprised to see that, despite the modern tendency of my novel, any reader can understand it and discern its nuances . . . It's turned out to be an interesting experience; right now I'm hoping that one of *El Espectador*'s paper boys will read it so I can get his opinion of it, and I'd like very much to know what the chauffeurs, shoe-shiners, and lottery ticket vendors think . . . I believe that the general public will like it . . . that it will be popular and that in this way it will prove that the contemporary novel can reach the masses . . . Anyone reading *Leaf Storm* can see that in the first chapter the author takes greater care to guide them through the monologues, so that it won't be hard to identify the character speaking at any moment . . . By the end of the work, the author leaves it to the readers to discover who is speaking on their own."

"How much time did it take you to write *Leaf Storm*?"

"About a year. Of course I'm not counting the first efforts that I just mentioned, from which this new idea emerged . . . But in that year when I was writing, even if I do know that I was in Barranquilla for about half of it and in Cartagena for the other half, I ended up spending the whole time wandering through all the towns along that coast, including those in the Guajira: even when I didn't know where my bags were, I always knew where I was keeping the draft . . . I finished it and mailed it to Editorial Losada in Buenos Aires along with *Backwards Christ* by Caballero Calderón, and one of the two were going to be chosen for publication. They chose Caballero's and after that the draft of *Leaf Storm* was in Argentina for almost eight months. I got it back with a note saying that my work demanded a lot of effort from readers, and that this effort was not matched by the novel's literary quality . . . The *Leaf Storm* I sent to Buenos Aires had three parts; it was longer, maybe double the length of what I ended up publishing. When I got it back from Editorial Losada, it didn't seem to have enough unity, I would have to rewrite it completely . . . I got rid of the third part, cut text here, added text there, such that in the end it was completely different. When I finally started talking to people in Bogotá about publishing the novel and they asked me to submit a draft, even then I wanted to cut more of it . . . I asked for a week's extension and got rid of a hundred pages more . . . I understood then that, during the five years I spent working on this novel, though I had thought that I needed to cut more, really there'd been something missing. And so you really have to write a lot, then cut, correct, tear many notebooks to pieces, before you can finally bring a few pages to the publisher . . . ! It's at this point that someone who doesn't have a true calling to be a writer gets discouraged and declares him- or herself satisfied with just one book . . ."

THE SECOND NOVEL

"Are you currently working on a second novel?" we ask him.

"Yes," he answers. "You see, the hundred pages that I mentioned a minute ago, the pages where *Leaf Storm*'s title came from, comprised something like a novel within a novel; the characters that paraded across those hundred pages that I cut from the draft only a moment before turning it into the publisher were not the same as the others in *Leaf Storm*; they seemed out of place there, even I couldn't recognize them as belonging to that first novel . . . Of course, the setting through which they move is the same one that belongs to the colonel, his daughter and her son; it's Macondo . . . But the thing is that I like that setting . . . Because it feels familiar to me and because I believe there's a special charm to it, an inexplicable and poetic mystery, what's happening in the towns, what they're getting the last of . . . Already the towns like Macondo are not the same as they were before . . . My second novel will definitely have the same setting as the first, as will any others that I write, if I write them; it will be set in Macondo . . . And you won't be able to call it a continuation or a sequel to *Leaf Storm* . . . It'll be like this, to explain a little more specifically: in my second novel I'm going to have some characters that live in the house next door to the one where the cadaver of the hanged man was left to sit . . . Those people, though they live in Macondo and are influenced by that same setting, will have different problems from the characters in *Leaf Storm*; you see how a distinct novel can be written, with the same setting and different characters . . . And that's why I believe that my novel is an example of *costumbrismo* . . . I think that those writers that in Colombia are called *costumbristas* tried to do the same thing I propose for myself, and that is simply to give local customs and characters an air of universality such that they can feel familiar anywhere in the world . . . I can better explain the concept I have of the nature of *costumbrismo* . . . *Quixote* is *costumbrismo* to me . . . By which I mean, I define *costumbrismo* as any work that fulfills that same purpose, that exposes the local within the universal.

"My second novel, which will definitely be out within

the next few months, will be titled *Los Catorce Días de la Semana* (*The Fourteen Days of the Week*)."[*]

LITERATURE AND CINEMA

We've gotten off-topic while relighting our cigarettes. He has been speaking very passionately. We feel the urge to take careful note of every word, every thought, but it's impossible. The ideas crowding into his mind are converted into agile sentences streaming out of his mouth. If he is really this eloquent, he is surely always a good conversation partner.

"I believe," he continues, "that the novel must have some purpose . . . Beyond being read by readers . . . The novel must have a goal, must contain some intention of the author's, distinct from the intention that it be read . . ." These last words convince us to share with him our thoughts when we learned, while following him into the elevator earlier, that on returning to Europe he plans to study filmmaking. We tell him that we think we see behind his impulse the same reasoning that brought the novelist Curzio Malaparte and the lawyer André Cayatte to direct films. These writers have come to believe that through film they can spread their ideas more efficiently. This is because the medium is accessible to the average contemporary person, who goes to the cinema to assuage today's universal need for diversion, and not just to the cult minority that reads books. We mention films

---

[*] The next work he published, in 1961, was *El coronel no tiene quien le escriba* (*No One Writes to the Colonel*).

like The Forbidden Christ and those directed by Cayatte, in which one finds not only technical excellence, but also an obvious attempt to convey certain concepts and ideas to the viewers.

TRAVELING TOWARD EUROPE

"Yes . . . That's definitely why I'm going to Europe," García Márquez says. "I'll leave Colombia next month and stay in France for a year to study film. I think I'll go to the film festival in Venice, before going to France . . . And already these days I'm not thinking as a writer but instead as a film director who can say in films the same things he says in books . . . Of course, the observation you've just made is entirely correct . . . If I want to be involved in movies, it's probably because I want to communicate my ideas to a larger audience . . . The cinema will enable this because more people go to the movies than read books . . . Of course this doesn't mean I'll stop writing, and if tomorrow I feel the urge to write a story I will write it—and, as I've said, I've almost finished my second novel."

"Which do you find easier to write—a novel or a story?"

"It's definitely easier to write a novel than to write a story," he replies. And then he adds, "Infinitely easier."

"What was the name of your first published story?"

"I called it 'The Third Resignation' and it was published in the *Fin de Semana* supplement of *El Espectador*, which was then edited by Eduardo Zalamea Borda."

"Who is your favorite author?"

"Sophocles . . . Yes, Sophocles, go ahead and write it down. And another thing . . . To me *Oedipus Rex* is the best murder mystery of all time."

"Why?" we ask him.

"Because in it the detective discovers in the end that he himself is the murderer . . ."

"In your opinion, which novel written by a Colombian is most in step with the trends of contemporary literature?"

"*Leaf Storm*," its author replies without any hesitation. This response hasn't come as a surprise. We already knew that there was no other Colombian novel like his; we asked our question only to confirm our own opinion of the work.

LEARNING SLOWLY

"Which Colombian writer has, in your opinion, the most authentic literary calling?"

"It's hard to say . . . Because in Colombia, writers haven't realized that the first thing they have to do is learn to write . . . If the painter must first learn how to wield a paintbrush, the writer needs to know how to write before attempting to publish something . . . But because that requires sacrifice, discipline, continuous effort, our writers get discouraged, they feel they cannot set aside the large amount of time that they all need to set aside if they want to learn to write . . . And because of this, in the end, those who consider themselves writers don't begin by learning to write, and so they convince themselves that they don't have a real calling, and they give it up. See, all writers have something to say, concepts to express, ideas . . . But, because they don't know how to write, they remain silent. That's what's going on."

"Do you think our literature is in crisis?" we ask him.

"Yes, I think it is . . . I think there's a crisis; we are, without a doubt, emerging from it, and there's no question that we'll eventually get out of it completely. About this, I'm optimistic because I have faith in the future of our literature . . . But first, our writers, if that's really what they are, will have to learn how to write . . . Otherwise we won't overcome our current literary crisis . . ."

"What have you thought of the critical response to *Leaf Storm* so far?"

"Much too generous . . ."

"In your opinion, how can local newspapers best support young intellectuals?

"By not giving them any encouragement . . . By not publishing anything of theirs that isn't truly great. Really we don't have to worry about opening the doors of the newspapers to young writers. When they write something great, the doors will open on their own . . ."

The telephone has just rung. Someone is speaking, and García Márquez asks her to wait five minutes for us to finish our interview, which has already lasted two hours. Before we leave, we learn that he studied law for four years and then was on the faculty for six months, but that he doesn't remember anything from those studies because he spent all his class time writing stories . . .

We shake the hand he offers us, along with a polite, wide, and sincere smile, as he says goodbye. We leave feeling that the author of *Leaf Storm* is a strong and vibrant person who truly merits the admiration of those who have had the pleasure to know him and hear him speak.

POWER TO THE IMAGINATION IN MACONDO

INTERVIEW BY ERNESTO GONZÁLEZ BERMEJO
REVISTA CRISIS, ARGENTINA
1975

TRANSLATED BY ELLIE ROBINS

It's been said that "Lenin and the Beatles are the two most important things to come out of the twentieth century." You could argue that Gabriel García Márquez, a synthesis of the two, is the third thing for Latin America. Now to find some new way to praise *One Hundred Years of Solitude*. I'll add just one thing, which I think is important: I believe that since the publication of that novel, we're much more aware of our identities as citizens of an enormous Latin American Macondo. Even Kissinger has turned to the novel in the course of his international Fu Manchu–style demagogy.

Since the coup in Chile more than a year ago—"a personal catastrophe for me"—he's given his life over to a noble obsession: supporting the Chilean resistance ("let's see if they start a revolution and I can get back to writing books"). If anyone proves that literature and activism aren't mutually exclusive, that in fact they're the opposite, it's him.

Now, as we walk with his wife Mercedes through the streets of old Stockholm and he observes that "Sweden smells like a first-class train carriage" and that "the Swedish are grown-ups even when they're very small," he makes up his mind to eat some "spaghetti at Michelangelo in the

Gamla Stan," since there's no alternative but to submit to an interrogation.

"Let's talk about literature," he almost begs, "I haven't done that for a long time." But after talking a little about *The Autumn of the Patriarch*, his film and TV projects, and the hundred stories he's writing in his free time, he'll be the one to return to Latin America; to the need to embark on a new kind of struggle, that of the imagination; and to Chile. Because he's the one who sent a telegram to "the murderer Pinochet" as soon as he found out that Allende had been killed, thinking that his fury might subside, "but as you can see, after all this time, my fury has not subsided."

GONZÁLEZ BERMEJO: Is *The Autumn of the Patriarch* coming out soon?

GARCÍA MÁRQUEZ: It's with the editor. It'll be out in April. It's four hundred and fifty typed pages, much shorter than *One Hundred Years of Solitude*, which was more than seven hundred.

GONZÁLEZ BERMEJO: We've been waiting for it for a long time. Onetti[*] said a little while ago—and he's not the only one to think it—that *One Hundred Years of Solitude* must have weighed heavily on you while you were working on *The Patriarch*.

---

* Juan Carlos Onetti, a prominent Uruguayan novelist.

GARCÍA MÁRQUEZ: Every writer must write the book they're able to write. *The Patriarch* was more difficult for me than *One Hundred Years of Solitude* because I find each book more difficult than the last; the literary process gets more complicated every time.

GONZÁLEZ BERMEJO: Why?

GARCÍA MÁRQUEZ: Because each book is a step forward.

GONZÁLEZ BERMEJO: Precisely: after the seven-league stride of *One Hundred Years*, the next one can't have been easy.

GARCÍA MÁRQUEZ: As far as my own personal process is concerned, *One Hundred Years* wasn't a larger step forward than the others. *No One Writes to the Colonel* took as much hard work as *One Hundred Years of Solitude*. For many years after *The Colonel*, I heard that I wouldn't be able to write anything like that again. I don't think of one book as being better or worse than the last; I just want to take that step.

GONZÁLEZ BERMEJO: Onetti also said that you needn't have worried about giving *The Patriarch* a different treatment than *One Hundred Years*.

GARCÍA MÁRQUEZ: But the subject matter demanded the treatment I gave it.

GONZÁLEZ BERMEJO: Let's get to the subject matter, then.

GARCÍA MÁRQUEZ: Many people have said that *One Hundred Years of Solitude* is a symbolic distillation of the whole history of Latin America. If that's the case, then it's an incomplete history, because it doesn't say anything about the problem of power. That's the subject matter of *The Patriarch*. And now we can change the subject; let's not talk about it any more, since you'll be seeing it soon.

GONZÁLEZ BERMEJO: Just one more thing: What did you discover about power while writing the book?

GARCÍA MÁRQUEZ: Many things. The thing is, when you write a book, you spend all day thinking about it. And I write my books so that I can read them.

My dictator says that power "is a lively Saturday"; he never finds out what kind of power he has; he fights for it every day; and toward the end, he says, "Damn it: the problem with this country is that nobody's ever paid any attention to me."

GONZÁLEZ BERMEJO: How old is the dictator?

GARCÍA MÁRQUEZ: Nobody knows; he was always very old.

GONZÁLEZ BERMEJO: Tell me a little about the structure of the book.

GARCÍA MÁRQUEZ: I can tell you that there's no dead time, that it goes from one crucial point to the next, that it's so tightly packed that a few times I realized that I had forgotten something and had trouble finding a way to get it in.

GONZÁLEZ BERMEJO: Is it a single movement?

GARCÍA MÁRQUEZ: I'd say it's six, but it's not difficult to read; you'll see soon enough.

GONZÁLEZ BERMEJO: What are your hopes for *The Patriarch* in terms of readership?

GARCÍA MÁRQUEZ: *One Hundred Years of Solitude* is about everyday life; I think that's why people were so interested in it. I don't know who it was that said that *One Hundred Years of Solitude* was the first picture of the intimate lives, the beds of Latin Americans; that's one of the things that grabbed readers most.

The Autumn of the Patriarch might have fewer readers, because the problem of power, at the level I'm approaching it at, doesn't interest as many people. Although who knows if that'll be the case, because if you think about it, the problem of power comes up at home, at work, in taxis, everywhere.

GONZÁLEZ BERMEJO: What's the central idea about power in the book?

GARCÍA MÁRQUEZ: The disaster of individual power; if individual power doesn't work, the only thing left is its opposite:

real collective power. But let readers decide: you've already made me say too much about it.

GONZÁLEZ BERMEJO: And after *The Patriarch*?

GARCÍA MÁRQUEZ: I can tell you with my hand on my heart that I have nothing more to say in a novel; I've backed myself into a corner. So I'm terrified that I'll wake up one day and have nothing to do. I'm looking for a job, do you know of anything?

GONZÁLEZ BERMEJO: I'm in the same position.

GARCÍA MÁRQUEZ: Until a job comes up, I'm working with Rui Guerra, the Brazilian director, on a film adaptation of "Blacamán the Good, Vendor of Miracles." We've found that that story allows us to give a complete cinematic account of colonialism in the Caribbean, from the Spanish conquest to North American imperialism.

GONZÁLEZ BERMEJO: I heard you were also doing something with Francesco Rosi.[*]

GARCÍA MÁRQUEZ: Yes, we've been working on an idea for a few years. Rosi and I are old friends, and in the interludes between films, he comes to Barcelona or I go to Italy to see him.

---

[*] Francesco Rosi was an Italian director and one of the central figures of 1960s and '70s Italian cinema. He directed film versions of *Christ Stopped at Eboli* and *Chronicle of a Death Foretold*.

I think we're nearly there now; what I can tell you in advance is that it will be a political film, quite an original discourse on imperialism—or at least, we think so.

GONZÁLEZ BERMEJO: Any more visual work?

GARCÍA MÁRQUEZ: For television. I wasn't very happy with the handling of the mechanics of La Violencia* in *In Evil Hour*. And now I've been given the opportunity—a rare one for a writer—to go back to it a little later. Now that I've had time to gain some perspective, and I think some maturity, I'm going to work on an adaptation of the novel for Colombian television, in twenty hour-long episodes. Little old ladies doing their knitting at three in the afternoon will watch something about La Violencia in Colombia, and whom it benefitted. And other people too.

GONZÁLEZ BERMEJO: Stories?

GARCÍA MÁRQUEZ: I have a hundred ideas, one for every spare moment I have left after activism for Chile.

GONZÁLEZ BERMEJO: I was struck by some statements you made on that topic in Rome, about the need for Latin American revolutionaries to enter into a period of reflection; you called for more use of imagination than of heroism.

---

* La Violencia refers to a period of civil war (1948 to 1958) between supporters of the Colombian Conservative Party and the Liberal Party. It was a brutal conflict that cost the lives of some 200,000 people.

GARCÍA MÁRQUEZ: We need to use our imaginations in Latin America, after so many years of ideological petrification, of swallowing things whole; the right already knows all our tactics.

GONZÁLEZ BERMEJO: What's the role of the writer in these matters?

GARCÍA MÁRQUEZ: Everything's about defining things these days, and some of the definitions are contradictory and bear no relation to reality. I think writers' political roles must be determined by the circumstances of each moment. When it comes to political work, writers like to be given concrete tasks. I must have done a good job on the Cuban Revolution for Prensa Latina, because afterward people said, "You're going to work here, on this front." I think I provided a good service in my work supporting the Cuban Revolution, too, and also now with the Chilean resistance. The Chileans have given me the great honor and privilege of allowing me to work with them, and I'm simply putting the enormous political capital that comes with my reputation as a writer in the service of the Chilean resistance.

GONZÁLEZ BERMEJO: What results has the support for Chile yielded so far?

GARCÍA MÁRQUEZ: The Chilean military junta mustn't be given any breathing room whatsoever, and it hasn't been. We've disseminated a bad image of them around the world. They did everything in their power to create that bad image all on their own; all we've done is make sure it's well known.

Results, you said? I think we've ensured that the Chilean government is viewed more poorly than any other on earth. Even the very governments that work with and help the Chilean military have to hide their cooperation as best they can. Pinochet himself has been offended by this "international lack of understanding."

We know that the things we're working on won't be the decisive factor in solving Chile's problems, but they're a very effective aid to the resistance working within the country, which ultimately will be the thing to effect change.

GONZÁLEZ BERMEJO: A little while ago I saw that a journalist had asked you which Latin American country you thought was most likely to have revolution in its future, and, I imagine to the journalist's surprise, you said Chile.

GARCÍA MÁRQUEZ: Well, after what's happened, it has the most organized, radicalized popular workers' movement, it has enormous international support and sympathy, and it has ever more unity on the left. Which other Latin American country has all that?

GONZÁLEZ BERMEJO: It's almost a year and a half since the coup in Chile. What has the junta done?

GARCÍA MÁRQUEZ: Taken power and repressed the opposition. That's all, apart from increasing inflation by two thousand percent and spending $500 million on weapons.

GONZÁLEZ BERMEJO: It seems obvious that they're getting more isolated all the time.

GARCÍA MÁRQUEZ: More lonely all the time. Something fundamental is happening, which I mentioned in the telegram I sent to the Chilean military on the day of the coup, and that's that "the Chilean people will never allow themselves to be governed by a gang of criminals on the payroll of North American imperialism."

GONZÁLEZ BERMEJO: Okay, let's talk about that telegram.

GARCÍA MÁRQUEZ: When I wrote it, in Bogotá, at eight o'clock at night, as soon as I found out about Allende's death, some friends told me it read like something from a children's book; it wasn't my fault that the situation was like something from a children's book. And I wanted to write it before my fury subsided; as you can see, a year has gone by and my fury still hasn't subsided.

GONZÁLEZ BERMEJO: Régis Debray told a Mexican journalist, not long ago, that he might not know what's to be done in Latin America, but that he does know what should not be done on the battlefield. Do you feel the same way? What are the things that must not be done?

GARCÍA MÁRQUEZ: One of the main causes of division in the Latin American left has been the eternal debate about the means of struggle. And the other is that some on the left align themselves with the Soviet Union and others with China.

Since these are causes of division, we must be very careful with them.

Choosing the means of struggle can't be done mechanically or in advance; what happens in advance is that the revolutionary movements that emerge in every country as cultural as well as political entities gain political strength.

The conditions themselves will dictate the best forms of struggle, and there's no reason they should be the same in every country. I want to get to the point where Che's failure in Bolivia isn't interpreted as the fundamental failure of armed struggle, and where the failure of the Unidad Popular in Chile isn't interpreted as the failure of the electoral route.

GONZÁLEZ BERMEJO: What about that other cause of division?

GARCÍA MÁRQUEZ: The answer seems to me to be that it shouldn't matter to revolutionary movements who supports one and who supports the other; that they needn't concern themselves with other countries disagreeing with them. That's nothing but a remnant of the old colonial mentality; the one that says we're nobody unless we have a mother country. And this way of thinking isn't the same as opposing international solidarity; not at all. It just means getting rid of the fear of the catechism.

GONZÁLEZ BERMEJO: In another interview you hinted at something about revolution and how to start it.

GARCÍA MÁRQUEZ: I don't know who the hell it is that's

ended up convincing us—the people who want to start a revolution—to accept the idea that revolution is apocalyptic, catastrophic, and bloody. We need to grasp once and for all that it's counterrevolution that's apocalyptic and catastrophic and bloody. You already know the figures: more than thirty thousand dead, thousands imprisoned, thousands tortured by the leaders of the Chilean military coup.

My idea of revolution is of the search for individual happiness through collective happiness, which is the only just form of happiness.

We need to put an end to the practice of martyrology that's emerged in Latin America. I want revolution for life, not for death; so that the whole world can live better lives, drink better wine, drive better cars . . . Material goods aren't inherent to the bourgeoisie, they're a human heritage that the bourgeoisie has stolen; we're going to take them back and distribute them among everyone.

Death isn't a necessary condition of revolution; revolution doesn't have to continue to be an inventory of disaster.

GONZÁLEZ BERMEJO: But blood might be unavoidable.

GARCÍA MÁRQUEZ: It might be; but if the revolution is bloody, that will be because the counterrevolution made it that way, and it will be as bloody as the counterrevolution makes it. The thing is to make sure there's no confusion about who's responsible, because it's those misunderstandings that scare our mothers. My mother doesn't understand how I can be a revolutionary if I can't even kill a fly, and I tell her that's precisely why I am one: for as long as there's no revolution, I live in constant fear that I'll be put in a situation where I have to kill a fly.

GONZÁLEZ BERMEJO: You've been becoming a powerful political man for a while now; you've even got Kissinger's attention. He told a meeting of international diplomats about a book whose human value had really struck him, even though he didn't agree with its author's politics, and he said that he hoped that Latin America wouldn't be condemned to a hundred years of solitude any longer. What do you say about that?

GARCÍA MÁRQUEZ: I think I ought to thank Kissinger for the clarification, because if he hadn't made it, people might have thought we shared the same political views.

But I must tell you something: a friend of mine asked an official very close to Kissinger whether it seemed strange to him that the author he'd cited in that speech wasn't allowed to enter the United States. I wasn't allowed a visa for twelve years, and I think the reason was my work for Prensa Latina in New York; then they gave me one again for two years, and now they're rejecting me again. I don't think you have to look very far for the reason: my activist work in support of Chile.

GONZÁLEZ BERMEJO: They must be worried about what you're going to do. Last time, you donated the ten thousand dollars you won for the University of Oklahoma's Books Abroad Prize to pay for defense for Colombian political prisoners. Speaking of which: Who are you going to donate your Nobel to?

GARCÍA MÁRQUEZ: My wife has totally supported my prize donations, but she's told me to remember her and my children next time. So I'm going to give the next one to her. And do you know why? Because I'm sure she'll donate it to a good political cause.

WOMEN

SUPERSTITIONS, MANIAS, AND TASTE

WORK

THREE INTERVIEWS BY PLINIO APULEYO MENDOZA
FROM *THE FRAGRANCE OF GUAVA*, BARCELONA
1983

TRANSLATED BY ANN WRIGHT

1. WOMEN

MENDOZA: You once had the good fortune to meet (was it at a cocktail party?) the most beautiful woman in the world. Apparently, there was a kind of *coup de foudre* between the most beautiful woman in the world and you. You arranged to meet her next day at the entrance to a bank. You kept the appointment, but just when everything looked set for something special to happen between you and the most beautiful woman in the world, you turned tail and ran. Just like a rabbit. Since she *was* the most beautiful woman in the world (you thought) it was bound to be more than just a banal affair and, as all your friends know only too well, Mercedes and your marriage are more important to you than anything else. Do we take it, then, that heroic sacrifice of this kind is the price to pay for a happy marriage?

GARCÍA MÁRQUEZ: The only thing wrong with your version of that old story is that the dénouement had nothing to do with conjugal happiness. The most beautiful woman in the world was not necessarily the most desirable, in the way I understand a relationship of this type. After a brief conversation, something in her personality just made me feel that in the end her beauty would not compensate for the emotional problems she could cause me. I've always found women to be incredibly loyal if the rules of the game are established from the start and if you keep faith with them. The only thing which can destroy this loyalty is the slightest violation of the established rules. Maybe I felt that the most beautiful woman in the world hadn't heard of this universal chess game and wanted to play with different colored pieces. Or perhaps I felt that, after all, she had only her beauty to offer and that this wasn't enough to start a relationship which would be good for both of us. So you see, there was a sacrifice, but it wasn't all that heroic. The whole episode lasted only half an hour, but it did leave behind something very important—a short story by Carlos Fuentes.

MENDOZA: How important have women been in your life?

GARCÍA MÁRQUEZ: You can't understand my life without appreciating the important part women have played in it. I was brought up by a grandmother and numerous aunts who all showered me with attention, and by maids who gave me many very happy childhood moments because their prejudices, while not fewer than those of the women in the family, were at least different. The woman who taught me to read was very beautiful and graceful, and I used to like going to school just so I could see her. All through my life there has always been a woman to take me by the hand and lead me through the confusion of existence, which women understand better than men. They find their way more easily, with fewer navigational aids. I've begun to feel almost superstitious about it by now: I think nothing awful can happen to me if I'm with women. They make me feel secure. Without this security I couldn't have done half the worthwhile things I've done in my life and, in particular, I think I wouldn't have been able to write. This also means, of course, that I get on better with them than with men.

MENDOZA: In *One Hundred Years of Solitude*, the women establish order while the men introduce chaos. Is this how you see the historical role of the two sexes?

GARCÍA MÁRQUEZ: The allocation of roles between men and women in my books was quite unconscious and spontaneous before *One Hundred Years of Solitude*. It was the critics, especially Ernesto Volkening, who made me conscious of it. I wasn't too happy about having it pointed out, because now I no longer create female characters with the same spontaneity as I used to. However, analyzing my own books in this light, I have found that it does in fact correspond to my view of the historical role of the sexes: namely, that women uphold the social order with an iron hand while men travel the world bent on boundless folly, which pushes history forward. I've come to the conclusion that women lack any sense of history. Otherwise, they could not fulfill their primordial function of perpetuating the species.

MENDOZA: Where does this idea of yours of the historical division of roles come from?

GARCÍA MÁRQUEZ: Probably from my grandparents' house,

listening to stories of the civil wars. I've always felt they wouldn't have happened if women didn't have that almost geological strength which enables them to face the world so fearlessly. My grandfather used to tell me how the men would go off to war, guns over their shoulders, not knowing even where they were going, without the slightest idea when they were coming back, and, naturally, without worrying about what was going to happen at home. That didn't matter. With only their strength and imagination to rely on, the women were left behind to keep the species going, to create new men to replace the ones who died in battle. They were like Greek mothers bidding farewell to their menfolk as they went off to war with the words "Come back bearing your shield or borne on your shield." Alive or dead, that is, but not defeated. I've often wondered if these attitudes, so typical of Caribbean women, aren't the cause of our *machismo*. Or rather, if *machismo* isn't a product of matriarchal societies in general.

MENDOZA: It seems to me that you're always attracted by the same type of woman—the Mother Earth figure designed for procreation and epitomized by Úrsula Iguarán in *One Hundred Years of Solitude*. But there are other women in the world (you must have met them) who are unstable, castrating, or simply flirts. What do you do with them?

GARCÍA MÁRQUEZ: These women are usually looking for a father figure, so the older you get the more likely you are to meet them. All they need is some good company, a little understanding, and a little love, and they are usually grateful for it. I say "a little" because of course their solitude is incurable.

MENDOZA: Do you remember the first time you were excited by a woman?

GARCÍA MÁRQUEZ: The first woman to fascinate me was the one I mentioned earlier, the teacher who taught me to read when I was five. But that was different. The first to actually excite me was a girl who worked in our house. One night there was some music in the house next door and, completely innocently, she asked me to dance with her in the garden. The contact of her body with mine—I must have been about six—was an emotional cataclysm I still haven't recovered from. I've never felt with the same intensity again or with the same sense of abandon.

MENDOZA: And who has excited you most recently?

GARCÍA MÁRQUEZ: I wouldn't be lying if I told you it was someone I saw in a Paris restaurant last night. It happens to me so often that I've stopped counting. I have this special instinct. When I walk into a place full of people, I feel a kind of mysterious signal drawing my gaze irresistibly toward the most intriguing woman in the crowd. Not necessarily the most beautiful, but the one with whom I obviously have a deep affinity. I never do anything, I just have to know she's there and I'm quite happy. It's something so pure and beautiful that even Mercedes sometimes helps me to locate her and choose the best vantage point from which to see her.

MENDOZA: You claim not to have an ounce of *machismo* in your body. Could you give us an example to prove this to any doubting feminist?

GARCÍA MÁRQUEZ: Not all so-called feminists have the same notion of what *machismo* is, nor do their ideas necessarily coincide with mine. There are, for instance, feminists who really want to be men and this defines them straight off as frustrated *macho* females. Others affirm their feminity by acting in more aggressively male ways than any man. So it's difficult to prove anything at all in this area. You can't prove it in theoretical terms, you can only show it in practice. *Chronicle of a Death Foretold*, to cite just one of my books, is certainly both an exposé and a condemnation of the basic *machismo* within our society—a society which is actually matriarchal.

MENDOZA: How would you define *machismo*, then?

GARCÍA MÁRQUEZ: I would say that *machismo* in men and in women is merely the usurpation of other people's rights. It's as simple as that.

MENDOZA: The patriarch is a sexually primitive man. His double reminds us of this as he's dying of poison. Do you think the fact affected his personality or his destiny?

GARCÍA MÁRQUEZ: I think it was Kissinger who said that power is an aphrodisiac. History demonstrates that powerful people are often afflicted by a kind of sexual frenzy, but I'd say my idea in *The Autumn of the Patriarch* is more complex than this. Power is a substitute for love.

MENDOZA: Yes, in your books, those who pursue and achieve power seem incapable of loving. I'm thinking not only of the Patriarch but also of Colonel Aureliano Buendía. Is this inability to love the cause or the effect of their lust for power?

GARCÍA MÁRQUEZ: The way I see it is that the inability to love is what drives them to seek consolation in power; but I'm not very good at these theorizings, which in my case are always *a posteriori*. I prefer to leave it to others who do it better and get a thrill out of it.

MENDOZA: The lieutenant in *In Evil Hour* seems to have sexual problems. Is he impotent or is he, perhaps, homosexual?

GARCÍA MÁRQUEZ: I never thought the lieutenant was homosexual, but I must admit that his behavior does arouse some suspicions. In fact, in one rough draft there was a rumor to that effect going around the town, but I took it out because it seemed too obvious. I preferred to let the reader decide for himself. There's no doubt about his inability to love, however, although I wasn't conscious of it when creating the character. I only realized it afterward when I was working on the personality of Colonel Aureliano Buendía. In any case these two characters and the Patriarch are linked through power, not through their sexual behavior. The lieutenant of *In Evil Hour* was my first real attempt to explore the mystery of power (at the very modest level of a small town mayor) and the Patriarch was the most complex effort. The relationship between them is clear. Colonel Buendía could very well have been the lieutenant of *In Evil Hour* at one level and at another he could have been the Patriarch. I mean that his behavior would have been the same in both instances.

MENDOZA: Do you really think the inability to love is very serious?

GARCÍA MÁRQUEZ: I don't think there's any human misery greater than that. Not only for the person afflicted but for all those whose misfortune it is to come within his orbit.

MENDOZA: Do you think there should be any limits on sexual freedom? What should they be?

GARCÍA MÁRQUEZ: We are all hostage to our own prejudices. As a liberal-minded man, I believe that theoretically there should be no limit to sexual freedom. In practice, however, I can't escape the prejudices of my Catholic background and bourgeois society, and like most of us I fall prey to double standards.

MENDOZA: You're the father of boys. Have you ever asked yourself how you would have been with daughters? Strict? Tolerant? Jealous, perhaps?

GARCÍA MÁRQUEZ: I've only got sons and you've only got daughters. I can only say that I feel as jealous about my boys as you do about your girls.

MENDOZA: You said once that all men are impotent but there is always a woman to solve their problem. Do you think our masculine inhibitions are as strong as that?

GARCÍA MÁRQUEZ: I think it was a Frenchman who said, "There are no impotent men, only unfeeling women." In fact, although not many admit it, every normal man finds any new sexual experience terrifying. I think the explanation for this anxiety is cultural. He's afraid of making a fool of himself, and in fact he does so, because his anxiety prevents him from performing as well as his *machismo* expects. In this sense we're all impotent and we can only come out of it with our self-respect intact thanks to a woman's understanding. This is not a bad thing. It gives love a special magic because every time is like the first time and each couple has to start from the beginning again as if it were their first attempt. The absence of this emotion and mystery is what makes pornography so boring and unacceptable.

MENDOZA: You sometimes missed out having a woman around when you were very young, very poor and totally unknown. Now that you're famous there are opportunities galore, but the need to keep your private life intact has turned you into that rare species—the man who's hard to get. Don't you ever feel resentful deep down that fate has treated you so cruelly?

GARCÍA MÁRQUEZ: It's not so much a concern for my private life that stops me being a public ladykiller, so to speak, as the fact that I don't see love as a quick lunge with no consequences.

I see it as a reciprocal relationship which simmers and grows, and it's impossible in my present circumstances to have more than one of these at a time. Of course I'm not talking about passing temptations which arise from vanity, curiosity, or even boredom and leave no trace at all, not even from the waist down. In any case, I've been pretty sure for some time now that there is no cosmic force capable of upsetting what you call the order of my private life; and we both understand well enough what that means.

2. SUPERSTITIONS, MANIAS, AND TASTES

MENDOZA: You said once, "If you don't believe in God, at least be superstitious." This is a serious subject for you.

GARCÍA MÁRQUEZ: Very serious.

MENDOZA: Why?

GARCÍA MÁRQUEZ: I believe that superstitions, or what are commonly called such, correspond to natural forces which rational thinking, like that of the West, has rejected.

MENDOZA: Let's begin with the most common examples. The number thirteen. Do you really think it brings bad luck?

GARCÍA MÁRQUEZ: I think it's just the opposite, actually. People in the know make out that it has a jinx (the Americans have been taken in, hotels there go from the twelfth to the fourteenth floor) so that nobody else will use it and they'll be the sole beneficiaries. It is really a lucky number. The same is true of black cats and walking under ladders.

MENDOZA: You always have yellow flowers in your house. What significance do they have?

GARCÍA MÁRQUEZ: Nothing awful can happen to me if there are yellow flowers around. To be absolutely safe, I need yellow flowers (preferably yellow roses) *and* to be surrounded by women.

MENDOZA: Mercedes always puts a rose on your desk.

GARCÍA MÁRQUEZ: Always. What's happened quite a few times is that I'm trying to work and not getting anywhere, nothing's going right, I'm throwing away page after page. Then I look at the flower vase and find the reason . . . no rose. I shout for a flower, they bring it, and everything starts coming out right.

MENDOZA: Is yellow your lucky color?

GARCÍA MÁRQUEZ: Yellow is lucky but gold isn't, nor the color gold. I identify gold with shit. I've been rejecting shit since I was a child, so a psychoanalyst told me.

MENDOZA: One of the characters in *One Hundred Years of Solitude* compares gold to dog shit.

GARCÍA MÁRQUEZ: Yes, when José Arcadio Buendía discovers the formula for turning metals into gold and shows his son the result of his experiment, he says, "It looks like dog shit."

MENDOZA: So you never wear gold.

GARCÍA MÁRQUEZ: Never. I don't wear a watch, or a chain, or a gold ring or a bracelet. You won't see anything made of gold in my house either.

MENDOZA: You and I learne something in Venezuela which has been a great help in life, namely, the link between bad taste and bad luck. The Venezuelans have a special word for this jinx attaching to pretentious people, objects, and attitudes. They call it *pava*.

GARCÍA MÁRQUEZ: Yes, it's an extraordinary defence mechanism that ordinary people's common sense has erected in Venezuela against the explosion of bad taste among the nouveaux riches.

MENDOZA: You've made a complete list of objects and things with *pava*, haven't you? Can you remember any of them?

GARCÍA MÁRQUEZ: Well, there are the most obvious, the most common ones. Big conch shells behind the door . . .

MENDOZA: Aquariums inside the house . . .

GARCÍA MÁRQUEZ: Plastic flowers, peacocks, those embroidered Manila shawls . . . It's a very long list.

MENDOZA: You also mentioned those young men in long black cloaks who entertain in restaurants in Spain.

GARCÍA MÁRQUEZ: The student musical groups. There are very few things with more *pava* than those.

MENDOZA: And formal dress?

GARCÍA MÁRQUEZ: Yes, but there are differing degrees. Tails have more *pava* than a dinner jacket but less than a frock coat. A tropical dinner jacket is the only item of this kind of dress which escapes.

MENDOZA: Have you ever worn tails?

GARCÍA MÁRQUEZ: Never.

MENDOZA: Would you never wear them? You would have to if you won the Nobel Prize.

GARCÍA MÁRQUEZ: I've already had to put not wearing tails as a condition of my attending a function or ceremony on other occasions. What else can I do—tails have a jinx on them.

MENDOZA: We also found other more subtle forms of *pava*. You once decided, for instance, that smoking in the nude did not mean bad luck, but smoking in the nude while walking about did.

GARCÍA MÁRQUEZ: And going around with nothing but your shoes on.

MENDOZA: Of course.

GARCÍA MÁRQUEZ: Or making love with your socks on. That's fatal. It can never work.

MENDOZA: What other things?

GARCÍA MÁRQUEZ: Disabled people who use their disabilities to play musical instruments. People without arms playing the drums with their feet or the flute with their ears, for instance. Or blind musicians.

MENDOZA: I suppose certain words have a curse on them too. I mean words you never use when you're writing.

GARCÍA MÁRQUEZ: Yes, all sociological jargon—words like "level," "parameter," "context." "Symbiosis" is a word with *pava.*

MENDOZA: "Approach" is another.

GARCÍA MÁRQUEZ: Yes, "approach." And what about "handicapped"? I never use "and/or" or "in order to" or "over and above."

MENDOZA: And do people have the same effect?

GARCÍA MÁRQUEZ: Yes, but it's better not to talk about them.

MENDOZA: I think so too. There's one writer who carries *pava* with him wherever he goes. I'm not going to mention him by name because if I do this book will be doomed. What do you do when you meet people like that?

GARCÍA MÁRQUEZ: I avoid them. Above all I refuse to sleep in the same place as they do. A few years ago Mercedes and I rented a flat in a town on the Costa Brava. We soon found out that a neighbor—a lady who'd come over to say hello—had *pava*. I refused to sleep there. I spent the day there but not the night. I went to sleep at a friend's house at night. Mercedes got really fed up about it, but there was nothing I could do.

MENDOZA: What about places? Do they have this effect on you too?

GARCÍA MÁRQUEZ: Yes, not because they bring bad luck in themselves, but because at some time I've had a premonition there. This happened to me in Cadaqués. I know if I ever go back there I'll die.

MENDOZA: You used to go every summer. What happened?

GARCÍA MÁRQUEZ: We were staying in a hotel when that north wind which really sets your nerves on edge started blowing. Mercedes and I spent three days in our room unable to go out. I had the sudden feeling, with absolute certainty, that I was in mortal danger. I knew that if I got out of Cadaqués alive I could never go back. When the wind stopped, we left immediately by that narrow, winding road. You known the one. I only breathed normally again when I got to Gerona. I'd had a miraculous escape, but I knew that if I went back I wouldn't be so lucky next time.

MENDOZA: How do you explain your famous premonitions?

GARCÍA MÁRQUEZ: I think they respond to bits of information or clues I pick up in my subconscious.

MENDOZA: I remember that first of January 1958, in Caracas, when you instinctively felt something serious was about to happen any second and, in fact, it did. There was a totally unexpected air raid on the Presidential Palace right in front of our noses. To this day I ask myself how or why you had that premonition.

GARCÍA MÁRQUEZ: It was almost certainly because when I woke up that morning in the hostel where I was living I heard the engine of a fighter plane. It must have stuck in my subconscious that something unusual was happening because I'd just arrived from Europe, where fighter planes only fly over cities in wartime.

MENDOZA: Are your premonitions very clear-cut?

GARCÍA MÁRQUEZ: No, they are very vague, like a kind of misgiving, but they are always related to something definite. Look, the other day in Barcelona, while I was tying my shoelace, I had this hunch that something had just happened at home in Mexico. Not necessarily anything bad. Just something. I was worried all the same because my son Rodrigo was leaving by car for Acapulco that day. I asked Mercedes to phone home. In fact something had happened at the very moment I was tying my shoelace. Our maid had just had a baby. A boy. I breathed a sigh of relief that the premonition had nothing to do with Rodrigo at all.

MENDOZA: Your premonitions and intuition have helped you a lot. You have based many important decisions in your life on them.

GARCÍA MÁRQUEZ: Not only the most important. All of them.

MENDOZA: All of them. Is that true?

GARCÍA MÁRQUEZ: All of them. Every day. Every time I decide something I do it intuitively.

MENDOZA: Let's talk about your manias. Which is your biggest mania?

GARCÍA MÁRQUEZ: My oldest and most constant mania is punctuality. I was punctual even as a child.

MENDOZA: You were saying that when you make a typing error you start the page again. Is that mania or superstition?

GARCÍA MÁRQUEZ: That's sheet mania. To me a typing error or a crossing out is an error of style. (It can also be simply fear of writing.)

MENDOZA: Do you have manias about clothes? I mean, do you have certain clothes which you don't wear because they bring bad luck?

GARCÍA MÁRQUEZ: Hardly ever. If it has *pava* I know before I buy it. Once, however, I stopped wearing a jacket because of Mercedes. She was coming back from school with the children and thought she saw me at one of the windows in the house with a checked jacket on. I was actually in another part of the house. When she told me this I never put that jacket on again. And I really like it, by the way.

MENDOZA: Let's talk about the things you like, as they do in women's magazines. It's amusing asking you the things we always ask beauty queens at home in Colombia. What is your favorite book?

GARCÍA MÁRQUEZ: *Oedipus Rex.*

MENDOZA: Your favorite composer?

GARCÍA MÁRQUEZ: Béla Bártok.

MENDOZA: And painter?

GARCÍA MÁRQUEZ: Goya.

MENDOZA: The film director you most admire?

GARCÍA MÁRQUEZ: Orson Welles, especially for *The Immortal Story*, and Kurosawa for *Red Beard*.

MENDOZA: The film you most enjoyed?

GARCÍA MÁRQUEZ: *Il Generale de la Rovere*, by Rossellini.

MENDOZA: Any other?

GARCÍA MÁRQUEZ: *Jules et Jim* by Truffaut.

MENDOZA: Which film character would you most liked to have created?

GARCÍA MÁRQUEZ: General de la Rovere.

MENDOZA: Which historical figure interests you most?

GARCÍA MÁRQUEZ: Julius Caesar, but only from a literary point of view.

MENDOZA: And the one you dislike most?

GARCÍA MÁRQUEZ: Christopher Columbus. He'

pava. One of the characters in *The Autumn of the Patriarch* says so.

MENDOZA: Your favorite literary heroes?

GARCÍA MÁRQUEZ: Gargantua, Edmund Dantes, and Count Dracula.

MENDOZA: Which day do you dislike?

GARCÍA MÁRQUEZ: Sunday.

MENDOZA: We know your favorite colour is yellow. But what shade of yellow?

GARCÍA MÁRQUEZ: I described it once as the yellow of the Caribbean seen from Jamaica at three in the afternoon.

MENDOZA: And your favorite bird?

GARCÍA MÁRQUEZ: I've said that too. It's *canard à l'orange.*

3. WORK

GARCÍA MÁRQUEZ: In general, I think a writer writes only one book, although that same book may appear in several volumes under different titles. You see it with Balzac, Conrad,

Melville, Kafka, and of course with Faulkner. One of these books sometimes stands out far above the rest so that the author seems to be the author of a single, primordial work. Who remembers Cervantes's short stories? Who remembers *The Graduate Who Thought He Was Made of Glass*, for instance? But that can still be read with as much pleasure as any of his major works. In Latin America, the Venezuelan writer Rómulo Gallegos is famous for *Doña Barbara*, which is not his best work, and the Guatemalan Miguel Angel Asturias is known for *The President*, a terrible novel, not nearly as good as *Legends of Guatemala*.

MENDOZA: If it's true every writer spends his life writing a single book, which would yours be? The book of Macondo?

GARCÍA MÁRQUEZ: You know that's not right. Only two of my novels, *Leaf Storm* and *One Hundred Years of Solitude*, and some short stories published in *Big Mama's Funeral*, take place in Macondo. The others—*Nobody Writes to the Colonel*, *In Evil Hour*, and *Chronicle of a Death Foretold*—are set in another town on the Colombian coast.

MENDOZA: A town with no train and no smell of bananas.

GARCÍA MÁRQUEZ: . . . but with a river. A town you can only get to by launch.

MENDOZA: If it isn't the book of Macondo, what would your one book be?

GARCÍA MÁRQUEZ: The book of solitude. If you recall, the main character in *Leaf Storm* lives and dies in the most absolute solitude. Solitude haunts the central figure in *Nobody Writes to the Colonel*—the Colonel waits, Friday after Friday, with his wife and his cockerel, for a war pension which never comes. The Mayor who fails to win the town's confidence in *In Evil Hour* is a solitary figure too. In his own way, he knows the solitude of power.

MENDOZA: Like Aureliano Buendía and the Patriarch.

GARCÍA MÁRQUEZ: Exactly. Solitude is the theme in *The Autumn of the Patriarch* and of course in *One Hundred Years of Solitude*.

MENDOZA: If solitude is the theme of all your books, where should we look for the roots of this over-riding emotion? In your childhood, perhaps?

GARCÍA MÁRQUEZ: I think it's a problem everybody has. Everyone has his own way and means of expressing it. The feeling pervades the work of so many writers, although some of them may express it unconsciously. I'm just another of them. Aren't you?

MENDOZA: Yes, I am too. Your first book, *Leaf Storm*, contains the seed of *One Hundred Years of Solitude*. What do you feel now about the young man who wrote that book?

GARCÍA MÁRQUEZ: I feel a lot of sympathy for him because he wrote it in a hurry. He thought he wasn't ever going to write again, that he only had this one chance, so he tried to put all his accumulated know-how into the book, particularly the literary techniques and tricks he'd borrowed from the English and American novelists he was reading at the time.

MENDOZA: Virginia Woolf; Joyce; Faulkner, obviously. The technique of *Leaf Storm* is very like that of Faulkner's *As I Lay Dying.*

GARCÍA MÁRQUEZ: It's not exactly the same. I use three perfectly identifiable viewpoints, although I don't give them names. There's an old man, a boy, and a woman. You can see that *Leaf Storm* and *The Autumn of the Patriarch* have the same technique and the same theme (attitudes to a dead man). The difference is that in *Leaf Storm* I didn't dare let myself go and the monologues conform to too strict a pattern, while in *The Autumn of the Patriarch*, I use multiple monologues, sometimes within the same sentence. By the time I reached this book, I could fly solo. I let myself off the leash and did whatever took my fancy.

MENDOZA: Let's go back to the young man who wrote *Leaf Storm*. You were twenty.

GARCÍA MÁRQUEZ: Twenty-two.

MENDOZA: You were twenty-two, you were living in Barranquilla, and you wrote the novel, if I remember rightly, working very late at night in the editorial offices of a newspaper after everyone else had gone home.

GARCÍA MÁRQUEZ: In *El Heraldo*.

MENDOZA: Yes, I know those offices—neon lights, ceiling fans, always extremely hot. Right outside was a street full of underworld bars. The Calle del Crimen—Crime Street. Do they still call it that?

GARCÍA MÁRQUEZ: That's right, La Calle del Crimen. I used to live there, in one of those hotels for casual customers which are really brothels. The room cost one peso fifty a night. *El Heraldo* paid me three pesos per column and sometimes another three for an editorial. When I hadn't got the one-fifty to pay for the room, I used to leave the manuscript of *Leaf Storm* as a deposit with the hotel porter. He knew that I valued those papers highly. A long time afterward, when I had already written *One Hundred Years of Solitude*, I came across this porter among the people who'd come to see me or ask for my autograph. He remembered everything.

MENDOZA: Did you have any trouble getting *Leaf Storm* published?

GARCÍA MÁRQUEZ: It took me five years to find a publisher. I sent it to Editorial Losada, a publishing house in Argentina, and they sent it back to me with a letter from the Spanish critic Guillermo de Torre advising me to concentrate on other things. He did, however, recognize something in me that now gives me a lot of satisfaction—a definite feeling for poetry.

MENDOZA: I think I've heard you say that something similar happened in France. With Roger Caillois, if I'm not mistaken?

GARCÍA MÁRQUEZ: *Nobody Writes to the Colonel* was offered to Gallimard a long time before *One Hundred Years of Solitude*. There were two readers—Juan Goytisolo and Roger Caillois. Goytisolo, who wasn't the good friend of mine then that he is now, wrote an excellent reader's note. Caillois, on the other hand, rejected the book outright. I had to write *One Hundred Years of Solitude* before Gallimard became interested in any of my books. But by then my agent had other commitments in France.

MENDOZA: Between *Leaf Storm* and *One Hundred Years of Solitude* (i.e., *Nobody Writes to the Colonel, In Evil Hour, Big Mama's Funeral*), your novels suddenly became realistic, restrained, more limited both in construction and use of language, and they contain neither magic nor anything outrageous. How do you explain this change?

GARCÍA MÁRQUEZ: When I wrote *Leaf Storm* I was convinced that every good novel should be a poetic transposition of reality. But, if you remember, that book appeared during a period of very bloody political repression in Colombia and my militant friends gave me a terrible guilt complex. "Your novel doesn't condemn or expose anything," they said. I find this notion very simplistic and mistaken now, but at the time, I felt I should involve myself with the country's immediate political and social reality more, and I moved a long way away from my initial literary ideas. Luckily I was able to get back to them. In the meantime, I ran the serious risk of getting my head kicked in.

Nobody Writes to the Colonel, In Evil Hour, and *Big Mama's Funeral* all reflect the reality of life in Colombia, and this theme determines the rational structure of the books. I don't regret having written them, but they belong to a kind of premeditated literature that offers too static and exclusive a vision of reality. However good or bad they may be, they are books which finish on the last page. I find them too limiting now. I believe I'm capable of writing something better.

MENDOZA: What made you change course?

GARCÍA MÁRQUEZ: Thinking about my own work. I thought about it a long time and finally came to the conclusion that it was not to the social and political reality of my country that I was committed but to the total reality of this world and the next without wishing to show favor or belittle any particular aspect.

MENDOZA: This means that, through your own experience, you have rebuffed the famous "committed literature," which has caused so many rifts in Latin America.

GARCÍA MÁRQUEZ: As you know very well, when it comes to my own personal political choices, I do have a commitment, a political commitment.

MENDOZA: To socialism . . .

GARCÍA MÁRQUEZ: I want the world to be socialist, and I believe that sooner or later it will be. However, I have a great many reservations about what came in Latin America to be called "committed literature," or more precisely the novel of social protest (the high point of this literature). This is mainly because I think its limited view of the world and life does not help achieve anything in political terms. Far from accelerating any process of raising consciousness, it actually slows it down. Latin Americans expect more from a novel than an exposé of the oppression and injustice they know all too well. Many of my militant friends who so often feel the need to dictate to writers what they should or should not write are, unconsciously perhaps, taking a reactionary stance inasmuch as they are imposing restrictions on creative freedom. I believe a novel about love is as valid as any other. When it comes down to it, the writer's duty—his revolutionary duty, if you like—is to write well.

MENDOZA: Having freed yourself from this commitment to an immediate political reality, how did you come to find this other—let's call it mythical—approach to reality which produced *One Hundred Years of Solitude*?

GARCÍA MÁRQUEZ: As I've already said, my grandmother's stories probably gave me the first clues. The myths, legends, and beliefs of the people in her town were, in a very natural way, all part of her everyday life. With her in mind, I suddenly realized that I wasn't inventing anything at all but simply capturing and recounting a world of omens, premonitions, cures, and superstitions that is authentically ours, truly Latin American. Remember those men in Colombia who get worms out of cows' ears by saying prayers, for example. Our day-to-day life in Latin America is full of this kind of thing.

I was able to write *One Hundred Years of Solitude* simply by looking at reality, our reality, without the limitations which rationalists and Stalinists through the ages have tried to impose on it to make it easier for them to understand.

MENDOZA: And the larger-than-life element, the exaggerated proportions in *One Hundred Years of Solitude* and *The Autumn of the Patriarch* and your latest stories—is that real as well or is it literary license?

GARCÍA MÁRQUEZ: No, disproportion is part of our reality too. Our reality is in itself out of all proportion. This often presents serious problems for writers who can't find words to describe it. If you talk about a river, the biggest one a European reader can imagine is the Danube, which is 1,770 miles long. How can the reader imagine the Amazon, which at certain points is so wide you can't even see across it? The word "storm" conjures up one thing for the European reader and quite another for us. The same applies to the word "rain," which cannot possibly convey the meaning of the torrential downpours of the tropics. Rivers with boiling water, storms which make the earth tremble, cyclones which sweep away whole towns are not inventions but the vast dimensions of the natural world in our hemisphere.

MENDOZA: So you borrowed the myths, the magic, the exaggerated proportions from our own reality. What about the language? The language in *One Hundred Years of Solitude* has a sparkle, a richness, a profusion which you don't find in your previous books, except for the title story in *Big Mama's Funeral*.

GARCÍA MÁRQUEZ: This may sound conceited, but in fact I've always been able to write like that. It's just that I hadn't needed to use it before.

MENDOZA: Do you mean to say a writer can change language from one book to another as you change your shirt from one day to the next? Don't you think language is an integral part of a writer's identity?

GARCÍA MÁRQUEZ: No, I think the theme of the book determines the choice of technique and language. The language I use in *Nobody Writes to the Colonel*, in *In Evil Hour*, and in *Big Mama's Funeral* is concise, restrained, and governed by a journalistic concern for efficiency. In *One Hundred Years of Solitude*, I needed a richer language to introduce this other reality, which we've agreed to call mythical or magical.

MENDOZA: And in *The Autumn of the Patriarch*?

GARCÍA MÁRQUEZ: I needed to find yet another language and extricate myself from the one I used in *One Hundred Years of Solitude*.

MENDOZA: *The Autumn of the Patriarch* is a prose poem. Were you influenced by your training in poetry?

GARCÍA MÁRQUEZ: No, by music mainly. I've never listened to so much music in my life as when I was writing that book.

MENDOZA: Which music did you choose?

GARCÍA MÁRQUEZ: In this particular case, Béla Bártok and all Caribbean popular music. The mixture of the two had to be explosive.

MENDOZA: You've also said that the book contains a lot of allusions and turns of phrase found in popular everyday speech.

GARCÍA MÁRQUEZ: That's right. *The Autumn of the Patriarch* is my most colloquial novel; it's the closest to the themes, expressions, songs, and refrains of the Caribbean. It contains expressions only a Barranquilla taxi driver could understand.

MENDOZA: What do you feel about your work in retrospect? Your early books, for instance.

GARCÍA MÁRQUEZ: I feel the rather paternal tenderness I mentioned before, the same thing you feel for children who've grown up and left home. I see those early books as faraway and defenseless and remember all the headaches they gave the young man who wrote them.

MENDOZA: They were problems you'd solve quite easily now.

GARCÍA MÁRQUEZ: Yes, problems which wouldn't be problems at all now.

MENDOZA: Is there a thread which runs through both those early books and the ones which were later to make you world-famous?

GARCÍA MÁRQUEZ: Yes, there is, and I feel I need to know the thread is there inside and still needs protecting.

MENDOZA: Which is your most important book?

GARCÍA MÁRQUEZ: *The Autumn of the Patriarch* is the most important from a literary point of view, the one which might save me from oblivion.

MENDOZA: You've also said it's the one you most enjoyed writing. Why?

GARCÍA MÁRQUEZ: Because it's the book I always wanted to write, and it's where I've gone furthest in my personal confessions.

MENDOZA: Duly camouflaged, of course.

GARCÍA MÁRQUEZ: Of course.

MENDOZA: It was also the book which took you longest to write.

GARCÍA MÁRQUEZ: Seventeen years in all. And I abandoned two versions before hitting on the right one.

MENDOZA: So it's your best book?

GARCÍA MÁRQUEZ: Before I wrote *Chronicle of a Death Foretold*, I used to say my best novel was *Nobody Writes to the Colonel*. I rewrote it nine times and it seemed the least vulnerable of my works to me.

MENDOZA: But you think *Chronicle of a Death Foretold* is even better.

GARCÍA MÁRQUEZ: Yes.

MENDOZA: In which sense?

GARCÍA MÁRQUEZ: In the sense that I did exactly what I wanted to do with it. This had never happened before. In my other books the story took over, the characters took on a life of their own and did whatever they fancied.

MENDOZA: That's one of the most extraordinary things about literary creation . . .

GARCÍA MÁRQUEZ: But I felt I needed to write a book over which I could exercise strict control, and I think I did it in

Chronicle of a Death Foretold. The theme demanded the precise structure of a detective story.

MENDOZA: It's very odd that you never mention *One Hundred Years of Solitude* among your best books when many critics consider it is unsurpassable. Do you really feel so bitter about it?

GARCÍA MÁRQUEZ: Yes, I do. It nearly ruined my life. Nothing was ever the same again after it was published.

MENDOZA: Why?

GARCÍA MÁRQUEZ: Because fame unsettles your sense of reality, almost as much as power perhaps, and it continually threatens your private life. Unfortunately, nobody believes this until they have to put up with it.

MENDOZA: Is it that you feel the success of *One Hundred Years of Solitude* is unfair to the rest of your work?

GARCÍA MÁRQUEZ: Yes, it's unfair. *The Autumn of the Patriarch* is a much more important literary achievement. But whereas it is about the solitude of power, *One Hundred Years of Solitude* is about the solitude of everyday life. It's everybody's life story. Also, it's written in a simple, flowing, linear, and, I'd even say (I've said it before), superficial way.

MENDOZA: You seem to despise it.

GARCÍA MÁRQUEZ: No, but since I knew it was written with all the tricks and artifices under the sun, I knew I could do better even before I wrote it.

MENDOZA: That you could beat it.

GARCÍA MÁRQUEZ: Yes, that I could beat it.

A STAMP USED ONLY FOR LOVE LETTERS

TWO INTERVIEWS BY DAVID STREITFELD
MEXICO CITY AND WASHINGTON, D.C.
1993 AND 1997

My first interview with Gabriel García Márquez took place in late 1993 at his house in Mexico City. He was just finishing Del amor y otros demonios, *a minor but charming work published in Spanish the next year and in English as* Of Love and Other Demons *in 1995, and was beginning to conceive a multivolume autobiography, the first and only volume of which was published in 2002. He was recovering from his first bout with cancer, a situation that fed his hypochondria and melancholy. The conversation, spread over two days, took place in a bungalow adjacent to the main house. Pleasant but not ostentatious, it was at once library, office and man-cave. It was very well heated.*

GARCÍA MÁRQUEZ: (*Points to the tape-recorder.*) Do we really have to use that? I'm an enemy of the tape-recorder. It has an ear but no heart. You could take notes.

STREITFELD: I write very slowly. So I'm afraid we must use it. Otherwise, this interview would last until next week.

GARCÍA MÁRQUEZ: Okay, then. I'm sorry I don't speak English. The biggest mistake I ever made in my life was not learning how to speak English perfectly. (*Gestures in surrender.*) Ask me what you will.

STREITFELD: You recently had a brush with lung cancer.

GARCÍA MÁRQUEZ: Yes. My prognosis is good. The tumor was benign. Well, it was malign but it had not spread. The doctors give me lots of optimism. I always said that if something like this were to happen, I wanted them to lie to me. So now they give me an impression that everything will be okay and I don't know if it's the truth or not. The check-ups remain terrifying. They might find something else. I recently had an appointment scheduled for Wednesday. On Saturday I was anxious. On Sunday, I thought I was going to die.

STREITFELD: What happened on Monday?

GARCÍA MÁRQUEZ: I moved the appointment up.

STREITFELD: Has the cancer affected your work?

GARCÍA MÁRQUEZ: I'm in more of a hurry. I used to say, "I can do this in twenty or thirty years." Now I know there might not be another thirty years. But I try to get over this when I sit down to work. Hurriedness in creative expression is immediately noticed. In any case, using a computer is changing me more than the cancer. The first novel I wrote on a computer was "Love in the Time of Cholera." I suspect it was the first novel written in Spanish on a computer by anyone.

On a typewriter I used to finish a draft and then give it to the typist, who would make a clean copy. It was a happy thing to see the new draft but the whole process would take a while. Now, with a computer, I just keep rewriting and rewriting. On a computer, a novel is infinitely correctible. It's so easy. You go on endlessly. But in the end it's faster. The proof is I used to put out a novel every seven years, now it's every two years.

STREITFELD: And yet you still have time for journalism.

GARCÍA MÁRQUEZ: Journalism is my true vocation. It keeps my feet on the ground. Otherwise I'm like a balloon, I float off. Journalism keeps me nailed to reality. Curiously, as time goes on, I find the professions of fiction and journalism merging. The essence of literature and of journalism is the credibility they create. People are convinced by details. They say, "That's it, it's right"—even if it's wrong. My new novel, which takes place in Cartagena, is about a legend but it's filled with reportage. I look for details. Once I've found them, everything starts to happen.

STREITFELD: You are famous both for the amount of research you do, and for not letting it show.

GARCÍA MÁRQUEZ: I am still looking for some sources that will tell me what kind of a job someone would have had in the Vatican library, and there are some points of medieval medicine I need to double-check. That's why I have all these books. When I saw Hemingway's library in Cuba, I could tell immediately what his profession was. A novelist has to be able to consult everything.

STREITFELD: And reveal nothing.

GARCÍA MÁRQUEZ: And reveal nothing. When you finish the novel, you should destroy all your notes and drafts. Magicians never show how the trick was done. A writer should be the same.

STREITFELD: (*Beginning to perspire.*) You like it warm in here, eh?

GARCÍA MÁRQUEZ: I can't think in the cold. Besides this house, I have an apartment in Bogotá, an apartment in Cartagena, a house in Cuernavaca, a house in Paris and a house in Barcelona. My friends laugh at me because they're all the same: white. I have the exact same computer everywhere, and the same temperature setting—the temperature of the Caribbean. Tomorrow, if I have to go to Barcelona or Bogotá, I just grab my diskette and put it in my pocket.

STREITFELD: Why white and not, say, blue?

GARCÍA MÁRQUEZ: When visitors see it's a white carpet, they immediately start to clean their feet on the mat. If it weren't white, they wouldn't bother.

STREITFELD: You were born in 1927—although some sources say 1928.

GARCÍA MÁRQUEZ: In my town, there were no civic birth certificates. I wasn't baptized until I was three. My father would say I was born in 1927. My mother said, "Let him be born whenever he wants to be born." Clearly, she's a practitioner of the new journalism.

STREITFELD: In either case, you're still a young man—not even seventy.

GARCÍA MÁRQUEZ: It's curious how one starts to perceive the signs of growing old. I first started to forget names and telephone numbers, then it became more encompassing. I couldn't remember a word, or a face, or a melody.

STREITFELD: That sounds grim.

GARCÍA MÁRQUEZ: I've sort of given up worrying about it. Everyone is at the point of dying in life itself. I want to write a short book, a manual for growing old.

STREITFELD: I've heard you get most of your ideas in the shower.

GARCÍA MÁRQUEZ: Yes, it's true. I work every morning, from about nine to two-thirty in the afternoon. Those were the hours in which my children were at school. But then I had the problem that I was thinking about the story through the afternoon and night. I realized I was thinking about my stories all the time, even when I slept. I'd wake up tired and bored.

So now from the moment I close the machine, I don't think about it at all until the next day.

I'm trying to develop a sports training attitude—I don't eat too much, only two whiskies at night. The first thing in the morning I read over what I did yesterday so I know what's ahead. I'm beginning to work out the day. I believe in inspiration—not in the romantic sense, or the Holy Spirit who determines what you write, but in the sense that I and the subject have an intimate communication. And then I get in the shower, and the ideas come.

STREITFELD: It sounds very efficient. How long are you in the shower?

GARCÍA MÁRQUEZ: Oh, ten minutes. But I would like it to be even more efficient. I want someone to invent a pill in which you take it and you've already showered, brushed your teeth. The bureaucracy of everyday things is so tedious.

STREITFELD: Doesn't the Nobel Prize get you released from many ordinary tasks?

GARCÍA MÁRQUEZ: The only thing the Nobel Prize is good for is not having to wait in line. They see you in line, they take you right up to the front.

STREITFELD: That's really the only thing it's good for?

GARCÍA MÁRQUEZ: Fame is like flying a jumbo jet, it's a very delicate business. Also, I can't complain anymore. The Nobel implies a sort of dignity. You can't say what you want to say about someone who is bugging you. Mercedes is now the one who runs the bureau of rancor. All wives run the bureau of rancor.

My life changed after *One Hundred Years of Solitude* was published, when I discovered that a friend sold my letters to a library in the United States. I gave up writing letters so no one else would do that. Fame is a catastrophe in my private life. It's as if you could even measure solitude by the number of people around you. You're surrounded by more and more people, you feel smaller and smaller and smaller.

STREITFELD: You have been famous for decades, ever since *Solitude* became an immediate sensation in 1967. You must be used to it.

GARCÍA MÁRQUEZ: I was famous but no one noticed. After the Nobel it was different. I had a project I wanted to do for a long time: Go to some small town in Colombia, get out of the car and write a report on what that town is about. But I realized something. By the third day, all the correspondents in Colombia would be there watching me do this. I'm the news.

STREITFELD: So you're turning to the past and writing your memoirs.

GARCÍA MÁRQUEZ: William Faulkner says something un-forgettable: that the best place for a writer to live is a bordello. There's a party every night, the best hours to work—the

morning—are always peaceful, and you have a very good relationship with the police. As a young man I was living in
a cheap hotel in Barranquilla where prostitutes would take
clients. It was the cheapest hotel in the city but I learned
things. Once I saw the governor—well, I heard his voice in
the hallway.

Faulkner was right. It was a good way to live. Every morning there was a big breakfast. I was very hungry then. This was
in 1950. The desk clerk was a very thin man, missing one eye.
A room cost about a dollar. I never got the same room two
nights in a row. Once I said I didn't have the money, explain-
ing that I was a writer, a novelist, and that meant I didn't get
paid well.

I showed him the manuscript—I was writing my first
novel, *Leaf Storm*—saying, "This is my life, this means more
than anything else. I'll leave it with you, and tomorrow I'll
come back for it." He said okay, and put it on the shelf. From
that day on, whenever I had no money, I would leave the
manuscript instead.

STREITFELD: That was when you were first reading Faulkner
and Hemingway. You've often spoken of your debt to them.

GARCÍA MÁRQUEZ: When novelists read another novelist's
work, they take it apart as if it were a machine. Nothing
teaches you how to write a novel except another novel.

STREITFELD: Faulkner gave you something else as well—a
sense that all of the Caribbean, whether his Mississippi or
your Colombia, was the same wild place.

GARCÍA MÁRQUEZ: I am a man of the coasts, not the interior, where Bogotá is. The officials, the serious people, lived in Bogotá. The coast got the bandits and adventurers. It is a synthesis of many cultures—Spanish, African, Indian. I believe many regions of the world are like this, full of wonder and mystery. Most people just don't see it. The reality is what is so fantastic. There is nothing magic about it. It's pure realism. I knew a woman in a small Colombian town who read *One Hundred Years of Solitude* and said, "I don't like this book. When you were with us before you saw much better, more interesting things than what is depicted here."

STREITFELD: In your short story "Sleeping Beauty and the Airplane," a passenger notices a beautiful woman and asks the ticket clerk if she believes in love at first sight. "Of course," the clerk responds. "The other kinds are impossible."

GARCÍA MÁRQUEZ: Yes, that's my view. The problem with love is making it last. There's a Brazilian writer I like to quote: Love is eternal as long as it lasts.

STREITFELD: You came from a very large family—I believe eleven brothers and sisters. That affected you in many ways. And you have two sons.

GARCÍA MÁRQUEZ: Do you know why we didn't have any more kids? We were afraid we didn't have the means to educate them. And when we could, Mercedes said she was too old. So I tell all recently married couples to have as many kids as they want. Eventually, you'll be able to support them.

STREITFELD: You are a great and controversial friend of Castro's. You've described him as a larger than life figure, who reads 50 reports a day, can be interviewed for 17 hours straight and eats 18 scoops of ice cream after lunch. He's a Rabelasian if not a Marquesian figure.

GARCÍA MÁRQUEZ: When I first knew him, I was at Prensa Latina, nearly forty years ago. I was his friend when no one knew who he was. We both have the conviction that Latin America's salvation is in its unity, and that the forces that prevent this come from outside Latin America. The destiny of Latin America is intimately tied to the United States. It's like a transatlantic ocean liner. There's first class, second class, all kinds of classes, but the day the boat sinks, everyone drowns. The sooner the United States realizes this, the better for everyone concerned.

STREITFELD: How close are you to him?

GARCÍA MÁRQUEZ: He comes to my house in Havana every time he can. He tells me everything up to the point of state secrets.

STREITFELD: People say you should be the Colombian ambassador to Cuba.

GARCÍA MÁRQUEZ: But if I were ambassador he couldn't come to my house. Aside from that, I'd be a bad ambassador. If they offer, I'll say no. I would say, I've been a cultural ambassador all my life, that's enough.

STREITFELD: I heard you bonded with Castro over literature.

GARCÍA MÁRQUEZ: We have this great affinity. We're part of the literary culture. He's a great reader. I bring him books—quick, easy books to help him relax. The first book I brought him that he really liked was *Dracula*.

STREITFELD: Your critics say hanging out with politicians is not going to be good for your writing.

GARCÍA MÁRQUEZ: When I first started to write journalism, everyone said, "Now you're screwed because it will take up all your time and you won't be able to write fiction." And that was when I was just getting started. When I started working in advertising for a while in 1963, they said the same thing. And again when I started making films. And again when I started talking about politics.

STREITFELD: They are particularly critical of your association with Castro, who is not a big champion of human rights. When there is a petition demanding Castro do something, your name is never on it.

GARCÍA MÁRQUEZ: I believe when people sign a petition, they make a great noise. They don't really care about the cause. They're just thinking about themselves—what the public is going to think of their petition.

STREITFELD: You have achieved fame and success that no living writer has managed. Why go on writing?

GARCÍA MÁRQUEZ: I think it's Rilke who says, "If it's possible to live without writing, do it." There's nothing else in this world I like more than to write. And there's nothing that can keep me from writing. That's all I think about. I think I write because I'm afraid of death. If I didn't write, I would die.

STREITFELD: Since you think about death so much, do you think about your funeral?

GARCÍA MÁRQUEZ: If I could control it, it would be just my wife, my children. I'd be cremated and that's it. Unfortunately I know it'll be like the funeral of Big Mama in the story—nine days of funeral rites, the president and the Supreme Court and the pope in attendance, the national queens of all things that have ever been or ever will be.

•

Four years later, I saw him again when he came to Washington, D.C., for a very rare U.S. public appearance. He had taken a break from his memoirs to publish News of a Kidnapping, *a documentary novel about the drug kingpin Pablo Escobar's war against Colombia. Based on scrupulous interviews—although not with Escobar, who was killed in December 1993—it took three years to research and write. We went to a popular bookstore cafe, where García Márquez's books were piled high but no one noticed that their author was right there.*

GARCÍA MÁRQUEZ: That piece you wrote about me—it was all about death. Young people always think the old are going to die at any minute. They don't know that the youth mortality is much higher.

STREITFELD: Something is the matter with your logic but never mind. Colombia seems in the process of self-destructing.

GARCÍA MÁRQUEZ: I never talk about Colombian politics when I'm outside of Colombia.

STREITFELD: Okay. So President Clinton is a big fan of yours. You're going to meet with him later today. What's on the agenda?

GARCÍA MÁRQUEZ: I never talk about American politics when I'm in America.

STREITFELD: Is death the only permissible topic?

GARCÍA MÁRQUEZ: All I can say is I sent Clinton an early copy of *News of a Kidnapping.* He got it on the sixteenth of the month. Five or six days later, I got a letter. It was dated the seventeenth. He said he read it all in one sitting, from beginning to end. He also said, 'Thank you for being the prophet of my presidency."

STREITFELD: I assume that is because of the comment you made that, if re-elected, Clinton would eventually be ranked as one of the country's great leaders. Were you just flattering him?

GARCÍA MÁRQUEZ: I said he's going to *be* a great president, and I still think he has the potential.

STREITFELD: In *News of a Kidnapping*, you write that Escobar "had employees who spent the day engaging in lunatic conversations on his telephones so that the people monitoring his lines would become entangled in mangrove forests of non sequiturs and not be able to distinguish them from real messages . . . [Sometimes he] traveled in a public minibus that had false plates and markings and drove along established routes but made no stops because it always carried a full complement of passengers, who were his bodyguards. One of Escobar's diversions, in fact, was to act as driver from time to time."

This all sounds almost as fantastical as the mad ruler in "Autumn of the Patriarch" selling the sea to the gringos, who take it away "in numbered pieces to plant it far from the hurricanes in the blood-red dawns of Arizona." Is it really true?

GARCÍA MÁRQUEZ: It's authentic. There's a journalist, a friend of mine, who was on that bus. Whether I'm working in journalism or literature, I'm always describing the same reality. There are some things about reality I don't use in my fiction because people wouldn't believe them. Escobar's employees were a hidden force that influenced the everyday life of the country that no one ever saw, up to the point that some people even doubted he existed.

STREITFELD: As Colombia collapses, there are again calls for its most famous citizen to take over.

GARCÍA MÁRQUEZ: When a country needs leaders, people look in the newspapers. They think anyone in the news qualifies. A tennis champion should become president, or so they think. Even Pablo Escobar thought he had the right be to be president.

STREITFELD: There are so many rumors about you, sometimes unpleasant. There was a story that Escobar gave you money to write your book.

GARCÍA MÁRQUEZ: That's a stupid thing to say, because I have more money than he did.

STREITFELD: He was a billionaire.

GARCÍA MÁRQUEZ: Okay, I'm not a rich man. I'm just a poor man with some money.

STREITFELD: You were also reported as saying you would not return to Colombia until President Samper and his corrupt cronies left office.

GARCÍA MÁRQUEZ: I never said that. In fact, I am coming here from Colombia. What I said was, I wanted to stay there without ever leaving again. Then I realized the political and social reality right now is so intense I couldn't write in peace.

So I went to Mexico, which the press interpreted to

mean I wouldn't come back as long as Samper was president. For me to say I'm not going to come back to a country while a president is in power is to do him an honor, an homage that I will not give to anyone.

STREITFELD: In the 1970s, you were widely reported as saying you would stop writing as long as Pinochet was in power in Chile. He was in power for 17 years.

GARCÍA MÁRQUEZ: I never thought he'd last so long. Even though you may think it's not true, I really am a realist. Time convinced me I was wrong. What I was doing was allowing Pinochet to stop me from writing, which means I had submitted to voluntary censorship. I was sacrificing something that even the Chileans living under him weren't doing.

STREITFELD: No wonder you try to say as little as possible in public. Someone always misinterprets it.

GARCÍA MÁRQUEZ: I always have the impression it wasn't exactly what I said. Maybe it's me. I'm such a perfectionist, so precise. When I can't find the right word, I get very angry. For three months I was blocked in writing *The General in His Labyrinth* because I couldn't find the right adjective. Then I found it—"*aulico*," meaning "relating to the court or palace"—and never even used it.

STREITFELD: Speaking of quoting, there was a piece about you recently in *The Paris Review* by one of the students who attended your writing school in Cartagena. She quoted you as saying, "Writing never stops being difficult. Staring at a blank page, one gets the same anxiety as with sex, always anticipating if it's going to work or not. There's always the anguish."

GARCÍA MÁRQUEZ: It's been many, many years since I had the blank page problem—not since I read the quote from Hemingway where he said he stopped in the middle of a page, to leave himself a place to start the next day. That does work. The student was taking notes from a workshop that lasted a week. It's really hard to quote well. I don't have that anxiety with writing, or with sex.

STREITFELD: Maybe I shouldn't have brought this up.

GARCÍA MÁRQUEZ: It's aggravating. One of the premises of my workshops is that journalism has to recover a sense of ethics. The only condition for the students is that they don't make the workshop into an article. All of them say they will not write about it.

That student in *The Paris Review* did not respect that commitment. She wrote that piece, and all the other students then complained to me. She could have written an editorial commentary on what the workshop is like, but what she did is just a transcription. That's the easy way to be a journalist.

STREITFELD: I liked one other quote from *The Paris Review* article, where you told the writers who had long sentences that you had to use "breathing commas."

GARCÍA MÁRQUEZ: My idea of a literary text is actual hypnotism. It's very important that the rhythm does not have any stops and starts, because when you have a stop or a start, the reader can escape. There are too many other books waiting. Any hurdle and the reader will go pick up something else. Commas may seem like a grammatical sign, but I use them for respiratory purposes. The reader must not wake up.

STREITFELD: I found a copy of one of your books in an edition I had never seen before. It was in Spanish, but it wasn't from any of your regular publishers.

GARCÍA MÁRQUEZ: It was a pirate edition. There are so many. The legitimate publishers are so hard to deal with that the pirated editions are always winning. But I'm somewhat grateful to the pirates, because I'm gaining readers.

Legitimate publishers are at fault for not competing with the pirates. The only difference between the two is that the pirates don't pay royalties. But the legitimate publishers hardly pay royalties either.

STREITFELD: What are you working on now?

GARCÍA MÁRQUEZ: I'm writing a trilogy, a three-part novel of 200 pages each. The common thread is love stories between older people. Is love different when you're old? I developed this notion in *Love in the Time of Cholera* but I am still writing so I can learn. In part I was inspired by Kawabata's *House of the Sleeping Beauties*. Usually when I read a book by someone else that is good, I am very happy and I admire the writer.

This is the only book I've ever read that has made me envious. I read it and said, Why didn't I think of this?

STREITFELD: What is it about?

GARCÍA MÁRQUEZ: In Kyoto there is a house where aristocratic older men can go see beautiful young women. They are naked but drugged. If the men touch them they wake up and it breaks the rules. So they can only watch—and the men discover the immense pleasure of looking without touching.

It's a beautiful book. One day I said, I am going to write something like this. The only thing I'm going to do is switch it to the Caribbean. The hardest thing is the fact that they're drugged. That's a very Japanese thing. It doesn't really fit into our culture.

STREITFELD: This story seems a long way from those prostitutes you used to live with back in Baranquilla.

GARCÍA MÁRQUEZ: In my story, the hero doesn't worry about sex anymore, because it doesn't depend on him, it depends on her. There's a French proverb: there are no impotent men, only women who don't know what to do.

It's flattery, no? Once, in Caracas, I said that all men were impotent. Women were thrilled. They said I was their hero.

STREITFELD: There is a stamp in Colombia with your face on it.

GARCÍA MÁRQUEZ: I hope it's only used for love letters.

"I'VE STOPPED WRITING"
THE LAST INTERVIEW

INTERVIEW BY XAVI AYÉN
LA VANGUARDIA, SPAIN
2006

TRANSLATED BY THEO ELLIN BALLEW

In February 2006, La Vanguardia's magazine published what was to be García Márquez's last interview, as part of a series of interviews with winners of the Nobel Prize in Literature.

In the immense human hotbed that is the Mexican plaza Zócalo—at once epicenter of the country's power and setting for the most diverse protests—where landless people from the country, homeless people from the city, and women fleeing their own husbands' violence can be seen camping out, several groups of indigenous people are purging passers-by of evil spirits in exchange for a few coins. We are tempted to engage their services, because in just a few hours our interview with Gabriel García Márquez will begin, a privilege few journalists have enjoyed since he was awarded the Nobel Prize for Literature in 1982, and we're tormented by the fear that at the last minute everything will somehow fall to pieces.

The cab driver knows the way to Pedregal de San Angel, a residential neighborhood built on top of volcanic rocks where movie stars, former presidents, and bankers have their homes.

After passing through the front gate and a quiet outdoor patio, we reach the living room, slightly out of breath from carrying the heavy Christmas gifts his friends from Barcelona asked us to bring along. Gabo and his wife, Mercedes Barcha, have lived here since 1975, when they left Spain, and have renovated and added onto the house continually. There are wooden beams, and countless clefts, windows, lace curtains, and apertures that let in the sun, illuminating, among other things, pictures of the writer's five grandchildren, whose ages range from eighteen to seven, and a gigantic yellow doll that resembles some sort of rabbit.

While we wait, we flip through the books sitting on his coffee table, some filled with portraits of Nobel laureates and others with Richard Avedon photographs (a little later, Gabo will tell us: "That Avedon . . . He came here, he took my photo, and within fifteen days, he died—I never got to see it"). We walk through a garden with many flowers—including some truly spectacular orchids—on our way to the private study Gabriel García Márquez had built. We catch him sitting before his computer, not in a magical moment of composition but rather reading the world news online. In a friendly manner, he asks us to take a seat and lets it be known that he is making an exception and only hesitantly submits himself to this interview because he hasn't been able to hold out under the pressure of those close to him; here, he takes us by the arm and asks, in a whisper: "So now come on, tell me, how much did you guys pay my wife?"

The first meeting, then, takes place in his office, and is interrupted only by a few strident English sentences pronounced by his computer, as though the CIA were periodically chiming in. Gabo's computer is the latest model and reflects every conceivable technological advance; it's been many years since he abandoned his legendary typewriter. "I had to buy a computer as soon as they came out," he boasts. "When I worked on a typewriter, I wrote one book every seven years, on average, and with a computer it's come out to about one every three years, because it does so much of the work for you. I have several identical set-ups, one here, one in Bogotá, and another in Barcelona, and I always carry a floppy disk in my bag."

As he speaks, he drinks Coke continually, an addiction superseded only by his need to be in constant contact with the news arriving by telephone, internet, fax, and mail about what's happening in the world right now, especially in his native country, Colombia.

Hesitant to speak about his private life ("for that you can talk to my authorized biographer, the North American Gerald Martin, who really should have already published the book—I think that he's waiting for something to happen to me . . ."), he tells us that "this year, 2005, I've gone ahead and taken a sabbatical. I haven't sat down at my computer. I haven't written a single line. And not only that: I have neither a project nor hopes of forming one. I never stopped writing before—this has been the first year of my life like this. I used to work every day, from nine in the morning until three in the afternoon, I used to say it was to keep my arm warm . . .

but really it was because I didn't know what else to do in the morning."

"And now have you found something better to do?"

"I've found something fantastic: staying in bed and reading! Now I read all the books I never had the time to read . . . I remember that before I would suffer greatly when for whatever reason I wasn't writing. I needed to invent some activity so I could live through till three in the afternoon, as a distraction from my anxiety. But now it's turned out to be quite pleasant."

"And the second book of memoirs?"

"I don't think I'll write it. I have some notes written, but I don't want it to just be a professional operation. I've realized that if I publish a second volume, I'm going to have to say things I don't want to say, because of some personal relationships that are not so good anymore. The first volume, *Living to Tell the Tale*, is exactly what I wanted it to be. In the second, I met a number of people that just had to come along and that—*caramba*, I don't want them showing up in my memoirs. It would be dishonest to leave them out, because they were important in my life, but they didn't end up being very kind to me."

Though Gabo doesn't give us any names, we can't help asking about Mario Vargas Llosa, the Peruvian writer who was a friend for a short period until, in 1976, he punched Gabo in public, here in Mexico, because of a personal incident that the two authors have left to be explained by "future biographers."

"You don't think it's possible that, some day, there will be a reconciliation?"

His wife, Mercedes Barcha, who came into his studio a few minutes ago, responds abruptly: "If you ask me, at this point it's too late. It's been thirty years."

"That many?" asks Gabo, surprised. "We've lived so happily these thirty years without ever having a need for him," Mercedes affirms, before adding that "Gabo is more diplomatic than I am, and so you can say those words came out of my mouth alone."

Returning to his unprecedented period of inactivity, the Nobel laureate clarifies that "my year-long sabbatical has ended, but already I'm coming up with excuses to prolong it through 2006. Now that I've discovered I can read without writing, we'll see how long I can make it last. I think I've earned it. With everything I've written, you know? Though if tomorrow I come up with a novel, how marvelous it would be! Really, with the practice I have, it'd be no problem to finish: I'd sit in front of my computer and churn it out . . . but people can tell if you haven't really put your guts into something. Over there behind me all the technological devices are turned on, ready to join in on the action the day that happens. I would love to come up with an idea, but I don't feel the need to sit down and invent one. People should know that, if I publish anything else, it will be because it's well worthwhile.

"You know," he adds, "I don't wake up scared in the middle of the night anymore, after dreaming about the deaths of the people from the stories my grandmother used to tell in Aracataca, when I was a little boy, and I think that these things are related, this and the fact that the ideas have stopped coming to me."

His latest "idea" to date was *Memories of My Melancholy Whores*, a short novel published in 2004 that millions of readers all over the world hope won't be his last. "It wasn't even planned," he reveals now. "Really, it comes out of an earlier plan; I'd imagined a series of stories like this one, all about prostitutes. A while back I wrote four or five stories, but the only one I liked in the end was the last; I realized that I couldn't get as much out of the idea as I'd thought, that what I'd really been working toward was that one story, and so I decided to throw out the first ones and publish the last on its own."

Another project he was working on, a project that has since been stalled, was the story of a man doomed to die after writing his last sentence. "But I thought: careful, it might happen to you . . ."

Gabo doesn't seem distressed by his creative drought, and instead views it with a carefree attitude that's very Caribbean. "My life hasn't changed now that I've stopped writing, and that's for the better! The hours it used to fill haven't been commandeered by any harmful activities."

The writer draws our attention to the large yellow doll we noticed when we first came in: "It was hand-made in Mexico, a gift from Felipe González,[*] who comes around here a lot." We then start to talk about his fascination with power, and the different politicians and ex-politicians that visit him. "As a writer, I'm interested in power, because

---

[*] Felipe González is a Spanish politician who served as Prime Minister of Spain from 1982 to 1996.

in it can be found all the greatness and misery of human existence."

He mentions his friendship with Clinton. "Have you met? He's a wonderful guy! I never have such a good time as when I'm with him. AIDS is what he's really worried about these days, he's sincerely shocked and disturbed by how little attention the authorities are paying to the alarming spread of the disease into new zones, especially the Caribbean. They're not listening to him, but nobody knows more than he does about the issue."

He takes us to see his home movie theater. "It's very difficult for me to make it to the normal screenings, I spend hours and hours giving out autographs at the door. This way they send the films here; otherwise, they invite me to private screenings."

His passion for the seventh art isn't new: when he was young, he even dreamed of being a director, a dream his son Rodrigo, a constant presence at prestigious film festivals like Cannes, Locarno, and San Sebastián, later fulfilled. Rodrigo, in addition to having directed episodes of *The Sopranos* and *Six Feet Under*, is responsible for the feature films *Things You Can Tell Just by Looking at Her*, *Ten Tiny Love Stories*, and *Nine Lives*. "It's a good thing they're so excellent," his father comments. "It would have been so horrible for me if I didn't think they were any good!" Rodrigo lives in Hollywood, and his brother Gonzalo lives in Paris. Both are currently staying with their parents, and they come and go as comfortably as they would have when they were children. Tomorrow, Gonzalo, a graphic designer and painter, will explain to us that "Gabo wasn't one of those dads that plays a lot of games with you, but he talked to you a lot, and was very open with us about 'grown-up' subjects. The kind of thing we'd do with him as kids was talk, and listen to music."

García Márquez's attempt to keep his private life private is more and more successful as time passes, and he seems to have prevented his fame from robbing him of time for his sons, his grandchildren, and his friends. In the beginning, however, "fame nearly ruined my life, because it disturbed my sense of reality, much in the way power does. It condemns you to solitude, creates certain difficulties in communication that isolate you."

Suddenly the phone rings, and the writer predicts: "It's Carmen Balcells, no question . . ." Mercedes picks up and, indeed, on the other end of the line the most famous literary agent in the world is speaking. The writer laughs heartily to himself: "See? The woman doesn't sleep. Nothing escapes her, she knows that we're talking to you right now . . . She has us under closer surveillance than ever."

Carmen Balcells has been working with García Márqez since 1961, when no one believed in the young writer, who wouldn't become an international celebrity until the publication of *One Hundred Years of Solitude* (1967), which follows the developments of the Buendía family over several generations, as they encounter several characters including a baby with a pig's tail and a priest that flies. It is now considered the epitome of magical realism.

Rather than walk through Mexico City, Gabo suggests that we transport ourselves mentally to another city, namely Barcelona in the 1960s and '70s, where he lived for a time and wrote *The Autumn of the Patriarch*: "We arrived in 1967 with a two-meter-long alligator skin that a friend had given me. I was ready to sell it, because we needed the money, but I thought better of it and in the end we decided against it. It had traveled with us over half the world, as a kind of token of good luck. It all happened very quickly. When I lived in Barcelona I went from having nothing to eat—before, in Paris, I had even ended up asking for money in the Métro—to being able to buy houses for myself.

"I don't think that city surprised us much," he explains. "It was as if we had already seen it. The reason I went there instead of anywhere else was Ramón Vinyes, that 'Catalan wise man' who made an appearance as one of my characters in *One Hundred Years of Solitude*. In the Barranquilla of my childhood, he'd so vigorously 'sold' the Barcelona he'd idealized in his memory, as an exile, that I was sure we had to go there." When they moved to Spain, Mercedes Barcha and Gabo left behind the cosmopolitan, refined, and progressive Mexico, and the various circles of filmmakers, artists, and literary figures, full of exciting personalities and activities, for a calm Spain that was then in the final stages of Franco's regime. Barcha fondly remembers "it was all a little snobbish, the Barcelonans were just developing *discoteca* nightlife while here in Mexico there were already hundreds of them! There they even put on sombreros when they go out!"

•

"They were trying to outdo Paris," recalls García Márquez.

"I've seen the show *Cuéntame** and that's exactly how it was: Gabo and I had arrived in that world," comments Mercedes, amused.

"It was as though there was some kind of covert loosening of morals, which centered around a *discoteca* called Bocaccio. To us it all seemed very old-fashioned," Gabo agrees.

Barcha points out: "They—the Barcelonans—thought we would be the ones who were out-of-date, since we were from Latin America, but it was completely the opposite. I would walk down the street in my pants or jeans and people would stare at me like I was something very strange. One day I asked Luis Goytisolo's wife, 'María Antonia, why are they always staring at me?' 'Don't pay any attention to it,' she told me, 'they do the same thing to me.' "

The restrictions of Franco's regime weren't as stringent in Barcelona as they were in Madrid, the locus of political power, and the Garcías enjoyed the proximity of France. Gabo recalls, "We'd go to France to see the films we discovered in Perpiñán, like *Last Tango in Paris*. Sometimes we'd go to Paris for three days straight to get caught up on everything. Barcelona was our door into Europe: from there we relocated to London (where we learned English), Milan . . . We went to concerts, foreign plays . . . I thoroughly quenched my thirst for culture."

Gabo and Mercedes experienced the bustling *gauche*

---

* A popular Spanish TV series about the last years of the Franco regime and the Transition.

divine,[*] the evenings that never ended and the early mornings at Bocaccio, the blossoming of new literary journals, the political tension preceding Franco's death . . . They socialized with other writers who'd been drawn to Barcelona by "Mamá Grande" Balcells, like José Donoso or Mario Vargas Llosa, and they were visited by Carlos Fuentes, Julio Cortázar, Pablo Neruda . . .

"Now I'm almost ashamed to say it, but those were very good years for us," Gabo says. "In the Barcelona of the early seventies, people lived really well, though you feel bad admitting it. Only now, when you take a minute to think it over, you realize how sad it all was."

Paradoxically, the Garcías left before democracy arrived: "We were in Bogotá when Franco died and, when we heard the news, we came back to Mexico. We thought that things were going to get very chaotic in Spain, that there'd be a lot of instability, and we weren't sure how the new Spanish government would react to *The Autumn of the Patriarch*, which was about to be published, and which narrated the decline of a dictator. I thought that they wouldn't believe I'd been inspired by Latin Americans, like Juan Vicente Gómez in Venezuela or 'Papá Doc' in Haiti, who ordered that all the black dogs in his country be killed because he believed one of his enemies had been turned into one, or Maximiliano Hernández Martínez in El Salvador, who had all the street lights in the country cov-

---

[*] The term for an intellectual and artistic movement in Barcelona in the 1960s and '70s made up of writers, publishers, architects, photographers, and fashion models.

ered in red paper to combat a measles epidemic. I don't know
how much sense this makes, but in the end Franco was for me
too modern and civilized to be the dictator I had in my head
and in my soul. You know, the best review of the book I ever
had was from Omar Torrijos of Panama, forty-eight hours
before his death, when he told me, 'It's your best book: we're
all exactly as you say.' "

Gabo has a house in Barcelona, and says, "I keep going
to that city, more or less every year, though my visit in 2005
caused too much commotion, because I hadn't gone in five
years. When we arrive, it's always as though we never left.
We wake up as if it were the most normal thing in the world,
and we go out to eat with people who've been our friends
forever. We go for walks and we watch ourselves grow older.
We walk everywhere. They stop you sometimes, they yell at
you from across the street, but with that distance Castilians
always maintain, keeping their displays of affection in check.
For example, we also went to Madrid a few times, where we
have a lot of friends, but we didn't stay because we're more
of a novelty there, whereas in Barcelona our presence has become quite commonplace. In Madrid, the word spreads to
the journalists, the singers, the movie people, it turns into a
constant celebration."

Gabo continues trying to avoid the spotlight. He believes subtlety is always more effective, even in politics. He's
maintained his friendship with Fidel Castro, but has distanced
himself "through silence" from his more dogmatic stances,
and has been instrumental in influencing the Cuban government to free political prisoners and soften their stances on
certain issues. He's been politically active in many countries,

in everything from the liberation of bankers kidnapped in El Salvador to getting dictators to allow family members of dissidents to leave the country. In the course of this, he's had several experiences worthy of a James Bond movie or one of the novels written by his friend Graham Greene. For example, in 1995, Juan Carlos Gaviria's kidnappers demanded that he assume the presidency of Colombia.* (The writer's response was: "Why would anyone choose to take on the responsibility of being the worst president of the Republic? . . . Let Gaviria go, take off your masks, and start promoting your ideas for change under the protection of the constitution.") "I have always been more of a conspirator than a 'signer,'" he points out. "I've always achieved many more things by trying to straighten them out from the bottom up than by signing protest manifestos."

One example of this covert diplomacy is that he now acts as a mediator for peace in Colombia, attempting to bring about some sort of agreement between the members of President Uribe's government and those leading the guerrilla group of the National Liberation Army (ELN). "Maybe we shouldn't talk too much about this, since it's still being worked out. It's not good to make declarations when you're in the middle of something. From the moment I was born, I've been hearing

---

* Juan Carlos Gaviria was the brother of César Gaviria, who served as president of Colombia from 1990 to 1994, succeeded by Ernesto Sampler. Juan Carlos was kidnapped in 1996 by the rebel group Dignidad por Colombia (Dignity for Colombia), and they did indeed demand that García Márquez take over Colombia's presidency from Sampler, whose campaign was believed to be financed in large part by drug traffickers.

talk of attempts to create peace in Colombia. Now, after much painstaking negotiation, they've finally agreed to have a conversation. I've participated in some of the first conversations in La Habana, and they went very well. I'm on good terms with both sides. These affairs, for a writer who's gotten used to success like me, are always very humbling, because in them so many different issues intersect.

"Violence has existed forever, and it's an ancient resident of Colombia," he recalls. "What's at the root of it all is an economic situation that only increases the gap between the very rich and the very poor. And there's so much money in the cocaine business, tons of money! The day they stop that drug from being sold, everything will get much better, because that's what made everything get so much worse. The biggest producers in the world are all there. So much so that now they're not fighting for political power, like before, but instead for control of the drug. And the United States too is completely wrapped up in the whole thing."

While posing for some pictures in the garden with his wife, Gabo says to her, laughing, "Now you see why I never give interviews, Mercedes. They start out seeming meek, and then they never leave. Now they're telling me to kiss you, what next? I bet they'd even ask me to say that I love you." It'd be a superfluous statement, considering that they met when she was a thirteen-year-old girl and are still there before us, sharing their lives.

Before we leave, García Márquez asks us which Nobel laureates will be appearing in this series of interviews: "Ah, I see that you've only chosen the good ones." Confidently, every once in a while he grabs hold of his interviewer and it's impossible to see on his face any of the legendary shyness that, in Barcelona, made him be silent and tremble terribly whenever he had to speak in public. "I think that I must have social anxiety, like the Austrian Nobel laureate Elfriede Jelinek, because I can maintain a one-on-one conversation, but it terrifies me to address an auditorium of people. My shyness? I have the great advantage now that the people who come here are already intimidated . . . and that makes it easier for me."

GABRIEL GARCÍA MÁRQUEZ (b. 1927, Aracataca, Colombia; d. 2014, Mexico City, Mexico) was a Colombian novelist, short-story writer, and journalist. He was one of the most influential and beloved writers of the twentieth century; his novel *One Hundred Years of Solitude* has been read by millions worldwide, and is the foremost example of "magical realism." His other books include *Love in the Time of Cholera*, *The Autumn of the Patriarch*, *No One Writes to the Colonel*, *Chronicle of a Death Foretold*, and a memoir, *Living to Tell the Tale*. He received the Nobel Prize for Literature in 1982.

ALONSO ÁNGEL RESTREPO was a journalist for the literary supplement to the newspaper *El Colombiano*.

ERNESTO GONZÁLEZ BERMEJO was the European correspondent for the magazine *Revista Crisis* and the author of a number of collections of interviews with major Latin American writers, including *Conversaciones con Cortázar* (1978) and *Conversaciones con Gabriel García Márquez* (1982).

PLINIO APULEYO MENDOZA is the author of novels, works of political criticism, and two books about his longtime friendship with García Márquez. He ran the Bogotá office of the news agency Prensa Latina with García Márquez in the sixties, and has been a contributor to *El Tiempo* and other newspapers.

DAVID STREITFELD writes for *The New York Times*. He was part of a team that won the 2013 Pulitzer Prize for Explanatory Reporting on how the economy is being reshaped by Apple, and he received a 2012 "Best in Business" award from the Society of American Business Editors and Writers for a story on a fake review factory. He lives near San Francisco with his family and way too many books.

XAVI AYÉN has covered cultural affairs for *La Vanguardia* since 1991. He is the co-author, with the photographer Kim Manresa, of the book

Rebeldía de Nobel (*Nobel Rebellion*), a series of interviews with Nobel Prize winners at their homes.

ELLIE ROBINS is a translator from Spanish who has worked in publishing in the UK and the United States.

THEO ELLIN BALLEW is a translator from Spanish and French.

THE LAST INTERVIEW SERIES

KURT VONNEGUT: THE LAST INTERVIEW

"I think it can be tremendously refreshing if a creator of literature has something on his mind other than the history of literature so far. Literature should not disappear up its own asshole, so to speak."

$15.95 / $17.95 CAN
978-1-61219-090-7
ebook: 978-1-61219-091-4

LEARNING TO LIVE FINALLY: THE LAST INTERVIEW
JACQUES DERRIDA

"I am at war with myself, it's true, you couldn't possibly know to what extent . . . I say contradictory things that are, we might say, in real tension; they are what construct me, make me live, and will make me die."

translated by PASCAL-ANNE BRAULT and MICHAEL NAAS

$15.95 / $17.95 CAN
978-1-61219-094-5
ebook: 978-1-61219-032-7

ROBERTO BOLAÑO: THE LAST INTERVIEW

"Posthumous: It sounds like the name of a Roman gladiator, an unconquered gladiator. At least that's what poor Posthumous would like to believe. It gives him courage."

translated by SYBIL PEREZ and others

$15.95 / $17.95 CAN
978-1-61219-095-2
ebook: 978-1-61219-033-4

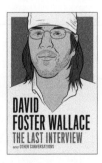

DAVID FOSTER WALLACE: THE LAST INTERVIEW

"I don't know what you're thinking or what it's like inside you and you don't know what it's like inside me. In fiction . . . we can leap over that wall itself in a certain way."

$15.95 / $15.95 CAN
978-1-61219-206-2
ebook: 978-1-61219-207-9

THE LAST INTERVIEW SERIES

JORGE LUIS BORGES: THE LAST INTERVIEW

"Believe me: the benefits of blindness have been greatly exaggerated. If I could see, I would never leave the house, I'd stay indoors reading the many books that surround me."

translated by KIT MAUDE

$15.95 / $15.95 CAN
978-1-61219-204-8
ebook: 978-1-61219-205-5

HANNAH ARENDT: THE LAST INTERVIEW

"There are no dangerous thoughts for the simple reason that thinking itself is such a dangerous enterprise."

$15.95 / $15.95 CAN
978-1-61219-311-3
ebook: 978-1-61219-312-0

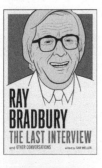

RAY BRADBURY: THE LAST INTERVIEW

"You don't have to destroy books to destroy a culture. Just get people to stop reading them."

$15.95 / $15.95 CAN
978-1-61219-421-9
ebook: 978-1-61219-422-6

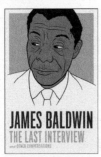

JAMES BALDWIN: THE LAST INTERVIEW

"You don't realize that you're intelligent until it gets you into trouble."

$15.95 / $15.95 CAN
978-1-61219-400-4
ebook: 978-1-61219-401-1